From Tuition to Promotion
Uncle Mike's Guide for the Recent Graduate
(and a Refresher for the Rest of Us)

Mike Spack

Yosemite
Press

To Jane, my foundation.

From: mbartlet@acme-associates.com
Sent: Tuesday, August 14, 2012 11:14 AM
To: gadams@acme-associates.com
Subject: **Chris Doe Emails and Quitting**

George,
One of my IT guys was cleaning up Chris Doe's computer since his last day was on Friday. Routine stuff, but Carl forwarded me a folder of really interesting emails Chris had on his desktop. They are a series of emails between Chris and his Uncle Mike about different business topics. I'm attaching an outline of the topics.

I believe we own all of the material since it was on a company computer. You should probably check with our lawyer.

There are a lot of great ideas in there and I think we should turn this into a handbook for our employees. I even learned a few things (by the way – we should talk about how we teach our new hires how to network).

I know you liked Chris and even mentioned you could see him replacing you as president of the firm in fifteen years. Now we know why he really left. I am a little surprised our monitoring system didn't catch this conversation happening. Maybe we could have figured out how to keep him here before he made up his mind to leave.

Let me know what you think and if you want me to do anything with these emails. I'm looking forward to our 10:07 tee time Friday.

Mark

Mark Bartlet
Chief Technology Officer
Acme Associates
50 South 6th Street, Suite 3245
Minneapolis, MN 55416
612-333-3333

Table of Contents

From: msmith@whiteowlconsulting.com
Sent: Sunday, March 15, 2009 3:14 PM
To: Chris@gmail.com
Subject: **Dazzle 'Em**

Chris,

The butterflies in your stomach won't go away until you get into the interview. That's good though. The adrenaline will help you focus. Don't drink too much coffee before the interview - you don't want to be jittery.

My first interview was a disaster. I didn't know anything about the company. I wore jeans and was really underdressed. I was late. Then, to top it all off, I somehow knocked over the bottle of water I was given. I spilled water all over my interviewer! He took a deep breath and stopped the interview right there. He ended up doing me a great favor as he escorted me to the door (I am lucky he didn't call a security guard) - he pointed out all of the mistakes I made and recommended I do some research on how to interview. I did the research he suggested and improved a lot (I couldn't have gotten any worse). We went over most of these ideas when you were going after internships, but a little reminder won't hurt.

We have been working on "your story" for several weeks now, so you should be comfortable with it. Being prepared is the key to getting your nerves to settle down once you get into the interview.

You've researched the companies thoroughly so you'll be able to explain why you are a good hire from their perspective. The important part of your story is explaining your accomplishments (in school, in your internships, and in your extracurricular activities). Be ready to explain that you didn't get perfect grades because of all of the other work you were doing. You want to show that you had a lot of other responsibilities and that you were a leader with your peers. Your grades were good enough to prove you were academically serious too. Don't sweat them.

Make sure you wear your dark suit, pressed white shirt, and conservative tie (I told your sister Amy to wear a skirt suit with conservative heels when she was interviewing). The only time you wouldn't wear a suit is if you were interviewing at a dotcom start-up and you knew they wore shorts and Hawaiian shirts. Don't forget to polish your shoes the night before and to wear a belt that matches your shoes (no brown belt with black shoes)! Once you are in your suit, don't eat or drink anything. You don't want to stain your shirt. Coffee has leaked out of my travel mug onto me on more than one occasion and forced me to change my clothes.

Stop at a McDonald's or a gas station on the way there and use the bathroom. Make sure you arrive in the company's parking lot fifteen minutes early, go through your materials in your head, double check your written questions (having written questions for the interview will show you are prepared), then go in five minutes before the interview appointment. Bring your questions in the nice portfolio your grandma bought you for graduation. Remember to take notes in the interview. It will reinforce you are studious.

Be super nice to the receptionist/secretary. Accept water with a smile if you are offered anything (again, no stains). Smile and say thank you a lot. The secretaries and receptionists are often part of the hiring decision.

Make sure you get business cards (at least names) of anyone you come in contact with so you can send handwritten thank you notes. Be sure to restate why you would be a good hire when you are writing to the interviewers.

Be prepared with your story, talk about your accomplishments, then sell how you are perfect for the position. Good luck!

Uncle Mike

Mike Smith • White Owl Consulting • 612-555-5550
100 Main St, #310, Minneapolis, MN 55411 • www.WhiteOwlConsulting.com

From: msmith@whiteowlconsulting.com
Sent: Thursday, April 16, 2009 8:29 PM
To: Chris@gmail.com
Subject: **Congratulations!!!!!!!!!!!!!!**

Chris,
I'm proud of you! All of your hard work has paid off.

It is awesome that you have two job offers in this down economy. It is interesting they both offered about the same salary and benefits (you've heard me say before that going for the money is important because your current salary always sets the stage for your future increases). With your goal of becoming an expert in your field - a true professional - I think you should take the job at Acme Consulting. Here's why:

There are two types of jobs a professional can have in their field:
1. You can be part of a backroom operation that is considered overhead by the company. Think of an attorney who is in house council or an accountant who works at Target. These are good jobs, but you shouldn't take them right out of school if you have a choice.
2. The better choice is to get into a company where money is coming in the doors because of your labor. You don't want to be seen as part of the company's operating cost. This means working in some type of consulting firm (law firms, CPA firms, architects, engineers, etc. all fall under this generic consulting firm label).

Two reasons to be in a consulting firm: One - when times get tough, it is easier to cut overhead than the people who are bringing in money. You'll have a more secure job. Two - you will learn A LOT more and you will learn it A LOT faster. When you are on the overhead side of things you do very routine work. Almost all of the unique work is sent out to a consultant. You'll learn a little bit if you manage the consultants or look over their work, but you are better off if you have to create the work product.

When I started at Bloomfield, the newly minted engineers were thrown out of the office to work as inspectors their first summer. I spent time watching/inspecting roads and traffic signals as they were being built. I learned how to read the plans and specifications, but more importantly, I was right there to see the mistakes that were made. When there were mistakes in the design, I was yelled at by crusty construction guys. Then, that winter, we "six month old" engineers did design work in the office. But here was the best part of the system - we went out the following summer and inspected "our" jobs and dealt with our own design mistakes.

It was an intense way to learn how my trade works. It taught me how things are actually built instead of just seeing the plans and then leaping forward to a fully built road. It's understanding what happens in between that makes a good engineer. This is true no matter what your profession. You need to understand the nuts and bolts before you can move onto the exciting work. You should figure out the technical equivalent in your field and land that job.

I'm not saying there isn't great value in having an in-house, overhead type job. Its fun and challenging to manage consultants. I had the in-house job when I worked for the City of Riverside as their traffic engineer. But to be good at the in-house job you have to understand what you are managing. Luckily I was about five years into my career when I went to Riverside. Moving away from the production line should be the second or third step in your career.

Don't be overhead, be a producer.

Uncle Mike

Mike Smith ● White Owl Consulting ● 612-555-5550
100 Main St, #310, Minneapolis, MN 55411 ● www.WhiteOwlConsulting.com

From: msmith@whiteowlconsulting.com
Sent: Friday, June 5, 2009 4:42 PM
To: Chris@gmail.com
Subject: **Re: What to wear?**

Chris,

Good question. I think you should wear slacks, a sport coat and conservative tie to work on your first day. You'll probably be overdressed, but you'll still fit in if everyone is wearing a suit. You can dress down to fit in once you get there. Take off the tie if no one in the office is wearing one. You could also take off the sport coat. If everyone is wearing jeans, ditch the coat/tie and roll up your sleeves. You'll look casual. What were people wearing at your interview?

Professionals used to have a uniform. This must have made life easier, especially for those of us who don't read fashion magazines. One less thing to think about as my fashion conscious cousin Lily told me as she explained why she liked the uniform at her Catholic high school.

If I was an engineer in 1955, I would wear a dark suit to work every day with a plain tie. If I was at IBM, I could only wear white shirts with that dark suit. Things are more complicated now with business casual (and compounded by casual Friday), let alone the anything goes dress at internet startups. My brain almost melts down thinking about the dresses, skirts, etc. the fairer sex throw into the mix. I think your sister Amy generally wears slacks or khakis with a blouse. I don't think she wears skirts or heels very often.

My advice is to be on the more formal end of what your co-workers are wearing. You'll look more professional, which is the goal. The bonus is that you'll feel more professional. I rarely wear a tie anymore, but I did almost every day when I started my career. Putting on a tie was a little ritual that made me feel more like a professional. It helped me act the part. Make sure you buy some good shoes. They're more comfortable, they last a lot longer, and they'll make you look sharper (no skateboarding shoes).

My general dress code is slacks, dress shoes, a button down collared shirt with the top button undone, and a sport coat. This allows me to fit into just about every environment. I won't look overdressed if others are wearing khakis and dress shirts (pretty typical business casual). I won't look underdressed if someone happens to be wearing a suit. I often take the coat off in the office, but I put it on if I hear a client is stopping by.

If I have a meeting scheduled with a bunch of people wearing suits (pretty much just lawyers these days), I will add a tie to my uniform. I also add the tie if I'm giving a presentation in front of a City Council or at a seminar. If I'm going to see a construction guy with his muddy jeans, I can take off the coat and roll up my sleeves. I also keep work boots and an orange safety vest in my truck for those rare occasions I have to visit a construction site.

Once you have a few days at your new job under your belt, you should be able to figure out a uniform that works for you. Think about what your clients or your boss' boss expects you to wear. Try to look like the professional you are.

Look sharp and you'll feel sharp.

Uncle Mike

Mike Smith • White Owl Consulting • 612-555-5550
100 Main St, #310, Minneapolis, MN 55411 • www.WhiteOwlConsulting.com

From: msmith@whiteowlconsulting.com
Sent: Saturday, June 6, 2009 2:48 PM
To: Chris@gmail.com
Subject: **First Day + Voicemail**

Chris,

You sound a little nervous to get started, which is totally understandable. You don't know what to expect on your first day in the office. The first day of my career started by meeting with an HR (human resources) person to go over company benefits and policies. Then I met the team I was assigned to and had a brief chat with my new boss. Finally, I was shown my new home away from home - my cube. I spent the rest of the day getting situated, which included learning about the phone system and setting up my voicemail. This is pretty much how the first day on the job went for me at my subsequent three employers and I'm pretty sure this is how your first day is going to go.

Make sure you get signed up for the company health plan. You are healthy and single, so I think you should go with the cheapest insurance option they offer if you get unspent money back. If there is no incentive for you to take the cheap plan, go with the one that has the lowest copay (how much you pay out of your pocket to the clinic when you go to see the doctor).

If the company offers a 401k or other retirement plan, sign up. Put in enough money to make sure you get the company matching contribution (if they have one). That is free money. It is good to get in the habit of saving a little bit for your retirement. It is really hard to get around to signing up later.

Here is a big decision for you on the first day – what to say on your voicemail recording (we all start at the bottom). Some people choose to just have their name prompt come up. Don't. This is your chance to make a good, professional impression. Also, don't start chatting so the person is confused into thinking for a few seconds that you are actually there. I recommend your voicemail says: *You have reached Chris Doe's voicemail at Acme Consulting. Please leave a message and I'll get back to you within 24 hours. Have a nice day.*

This might sound like overkill, but trust me on this, you should write out your voicemail message so you can read it into the phone. If you wing it, your message will sound like you winged it.

I think it is a waste of time to change your voicemail every day. I don't care if you'll be out of the office from 10:00 to 11:00 a.m. getting a pedicure. You don't need to tell me. I also don't want you lecturing me about how to leave a message (i.e. leave your name, number - slowly, and a brief message along with your favorite color and Zodiac sign). If you are going to be out of the office and not able to respond within 24 hours, change your message to say: *You have reached Chris Doe's voicemail at Acme Consulting. I'm out of the office and will be returning calls on June 8th. Please leave a message and I'll get back to you then. If this is an urgent matter, please press zero and ask for Jim Johnson* (your boss) *who will be able to assist you. Have a nice day.*

When you change your message, the first thing you should do when you get back into the office is change your voicemail back to your generic message. Put this on your calendar so you don't forget! It is pretty unprofessional to hear a message saying someone will be back.....yesterday.

Sign up for all of the company benefits on your first day and get your voicemail setup right.

Uncle Mike

Mike Smith ● White Owl Consulting ● 612-555-5550
100 Main St, #310, Minneapolis, MN 55411 ● www.WhiteOwlConsulting.com

From: msmith@whiteowlconsulting.com
Sent: Tuesday, June 9, 2009 8:39 PM
To: Chris@gmail.com
Subject: **Voicemail Continued**

Chris,
How does it feel to be in the working world? It took me several weeks at my first job to get used to sitting in a cube from 9 to 5. It was very different from going to classes.

I forgot to mention a few things about voicemail in my last email to you. Here are a few more thoughts.

Develop the rigid habit of returning calls within 24 hours, if not before the end of the day that you get the call. It must be important if someone took the time to call you and leave a message. It's arrogant to think you are so important you can get back to that person in a few days. Plus it is easier to knock out the phone call when it is fresh in both your minds.

We covered the Yin of voicemail (your mailbox message), but we didn't cover the Yang (leaving a voicemail message). First, before you make the call, think for thirty seconds about why you're calling and prepare (your uncle Ted is going to tell me I'm being very Zen like). Shut the trade magazine and your email. It's even a good practice to turn off the computer monitor while you are on the phone so you aren't tempted to look at things (unless you need to look up a document).

Part of your preparation should be a one sentence purpose for your call. If the person answers the phone, you should say "*Hi Joan, this is Chris Doe at Acme Consulting* (they'll probably say something pleasant like Hi Chris)." Then you can follow-up with your reason for calling.

It's pretty similar if it rings through to their voicemail. You say:
   "*Hi Joan, this is Chris Doe at Acme Consulting. My number is 952-555-5309. Please call me back about the xxxx matter. Again this is Chris Doe at 952-555-5309. Thanks.*"

A few things about the voicemail - say your name and number slowly so Joan can write it down. This helps Joan if she needs to replay the message (it sucks to have to re-listen to a two minute voicemail because the person put their phone number last and you didn't get all of the digits the first time you listened). You put your name and number first so Joan probably wrote down part of it as she was listening. Close with your name and number to give Joan a second chance to get the whole thing. Please make sure your message is only 20 to 30 seconds long - easy to do if you're prepared.

Finally, speak clearly. I have received voicemails that I couldn't understand (maybe they were eating when they called). Needless to say, I couldn't call them back which is the whole purpose of voicemail.

Be prepared for your phone calls – don't wing 'em.

Uncle Mike

Mike Smith • White Owl Consulting • 612-555-5550
100 Main St, #310, Minneapolis, MN 55411 • www.WhiteOwlConsulting.com

From: msmith@whiteowlconsulting.com
Sent: Tuesday, July 7, 2009 2:13PM
To: cdoe@acme-associates.com
Subject: **Caring**

Chris,

It was good to see you at the 4th of July picnic. We enjoyed meeting Heather. Are you sure it was wise to introduce her to your crazy family after only dating for a few months?

I thought I'd try your work email address to make sure I got it right. I had a few beers at the picnic by the time you gave me your new email address.

I just had to fire an employee. These are the worst kind of days for me. I like him, but he just didn't seem to care about his work. He always had an excuse, but his lack of follow-through was just too consistent. I hope he lands on his feet. Working here wasn't the right fit for him.

I think you care about your work. You need to in order to be a true professional. And more important – you need to get satisfaction from your career. (I say this often – your company is incapable of loving you. But you should still get satisfaction from your projects, care about your co-workers, and care about your clients. Just don't count on the company always being there for you. Look out for yourself.)

Caring about your work is important. It will help you survive layoffs. It will help you rise in the company faster. It will help you make more money. It will help you gain more interesting projects than your peers.

Care by being a problem solver. Be at the heart of how your company makes money (the primary purpose of all companies).

If you don't care about your work, find different work.

Uncle Mike

Mike Smith ● White Owl Consulting ● 612-555-5550
100 Main St, #310, Minneapolis, MN 55411 ● www.WhiteOwlConsulting.com

From: msmith@whiteowlconsulting.com
Sent: Sunday, July 26, 2009 1:42 PM
To: cdoe@acme-associates.com
Subject: **<u>Paycheck John</u>**

Chris,

I'm up at the cabin. The fishing isn't so good. It's too hot. Are you going to be able to come up for a weekend before the end of the summer? I think your dad is coming up to do some fishing in September.

So you've run up against Paycheck John. Most offices have at least one. They are usually low to mid-level guys who have been with the company a long time. They've been doing the same job for decades and you better not suggest there is a better way of doing things.

The first thing I want you to do is slow down. Think of yourself as a newly minted doctor – a resident. After passing the boards, doctors spend their first few years in learning mode. They spend a lot of time learning how to diagnose problems before they start recommending procedures. You might have a suggestion or two for your boss during your first year, but you should largely be watching and learning. You wouldn't expect a resident to come in, see a patient for two minutes, tell them they have non-Hodgkin's Lymphoma, and start them on chemo-therapy next week. There is a protocol to making changes.

Don't worry too much about what you have already done. I came into Bloomfield with a high opinion of myself. They had a questionnaire for new employees to fill out and I remember offering to help with personnel decisions since I had so much leadership experience in college. I am embarrassed at how naïve I was, but it didn't really hurt my career (even though my boss John – not Paycheck John - asked me if I wanted him to clear out a corner office for me).

You still need to deal with Paycheck John. Try to learn what he does without getting sucked into his bad habits. Learn what your boss expects of Paycheck John. You aren't his supervisor, so don't spend too much mental anguish on what he does and does not do.

When you do come up with an idea about changing something your department does, bring it up with your boss. Spend a lot of time thinking through the angles. Try to figure out how the old way got implemented.

Figure out what has changed (new software, internet, new technology, etc.) so you can explain why you think a change is needed without being offensive. The original process may have been set up by your boss. The last thing you want to do is call something stupid. Don't offend anyone with your suggestion. Just bring up the idea casually with your boss the next time you have a discussion. If he seems open to the idea, offer to put together a memo on the topic that would describe the change along with the benefits and risks.

Listen, learn, question, and then diagnose.

Uncle Mike

Mike Smith ● White Owl Consulting ● 612-555-5550
100 Main St, #310, Minneapolis, MN 55411 ● www.WhiteOwlConsulting.com

From: msmith@whiteowlconsulting.com
Sent: Saturday, August 8, 2009 8:12 AM
To: cdoe@acme-associates.com
Subject: **Using Outlook**

Chris,

It took me longer than it should have to figure out "CM" meant you wanted me to call you. Remember, I grew up in the Stone Age (B4 cell phones). I know you text a lot and think I'm old fashioned, but you need to write your emails so even your grandpa could understand them. It's part of being a professional working across generations. By the way (or BTW) – do you want to golf on Saturday the 15th? I have an opening in my foursome. Our tee time is 8:14 a.m.

My introduction to work email was a little traumatic. A few weeks into my college internship my boss called me over to look at his computer. The city was just starting to use email and he showed me how it worked. Even though I was in engineering at the University of Minnesota (which was an early pioneer with the internet), I had not used email yet. I don't remember the details of what he wanted me to do or why emailing from his computer was the way to do it, but I do remember what happened.

Somehow I sent an email to every employee in the City of St. Paul who had an email address. My boss was inundated with reply emails asking what the email was about and why they received it. Not bright. Based on this and other painful experiences, here are some thoughts on using Outlook.

One - learn how to put a delay on your outgoing email. Microsoft Outlook has the feature, so every email program in the world must have it. Basically, the delay gives you time (I set mine up for 60 seconds) from when you hit the send button to when the message actually hits cyberspace. About every two weeks I grab a message that is sitting in this 60 second limbo. I've caught typos, sending the message to the wrong email address, and the big one - not attaching the promised attachments. This delay will save you from several embarrassments a year.

Two - have a signature on your email that goes on every new email AND every response you send. It should include your name, company, phone number, and address. You can add an informal "Chris" at the bottom of your text ahead of your signature if you want it to be less formal. It's easier to sort through my inbox to find someone's phone number or address than to go through my contact lists (ok I'm a lazy slug who doesn't keep my contact list fully up to date). But your client may be a lazy slug like me and you shouldn't give them a reason to be annoyed with you. DO NOT use funky graphics or potentially offensive quotes/sayings with your signature block. Remember, you are a professional.

Three - don't use a vacation notice. You should actively send out an email to the people you are working with a few days before you leave. A heads up to get in any last minute requests. You should also let them know who to contact if they have an emergency (your boss?). If you are a very important person, you should have one of your co-workers go through your email to pull out the urgent items. They should respond, offering to help in your absence. The automatic "out of the office" notice gives very poor customer service.

Learn how to use your email software.

Uncle Mike

Mike Smith ● White Owl Consulting ● 612-555-5550
100 Main St, #310, Minneapolis, MN 55411 ● www.WhiteOwlConsulting.com

From: msmith@whiteowlconsulting.com
Sent: Tuesday, August 25, 2009 11:15 AM
To: cdoe@acme-associates.com
Subject: **Grunt Work**

Chris,
I still can't believe you took all of our money on the golf course a few weeks ago. That was an amazing putt you made on the 17th hole. Your game has improved a lot.

Sorry you aren't working on anything exciting yet. Trust me, things will get better. One of my first tasks in my career was to go out and manually count cars. I'm not sure what grunt work looks like in your profession, but counting cars is the definition of grunt work for traffic engineers. Its work that has to get done, but it rolls down hill to the junior staff very fast. Architects come out of school dreaming of designing skyscrapers. They may have even done some great sketches in architecture school. Reality is they start out writing specifications for light fixtures. We all start at the bottom.

Grunt work gets boring really fast. It's easy to think the work is beneath you, but you need to change your attitude. This grunt work is part of your education and it has to get done right. How are you going to manage and make sure this grunt work is done properly in the future if you have never done it yourself?

Also, bosses notice the little things. Taking pride in all of your work, no matter how boring, will tell your boss a lot about your character.

Two things about my grunt work - counting cars. First, it was very good at giving me a feel for how intersections operate. I would do a count, take the data back to the office, plug it into the software models and analyze it. After doing this a couple of dozen times, I was able to get a gut feel for operations. Now I can go watch an intersection for fifteen minutes and have a pretty good idea how it is operating without going back and running through the models. This is a foundational skill for my industry.

Second, part of my business is managing car counting projects for other engineers. I have carved out a niche by doing the grunt work the other engineering firms and government agencies don't like to do. Doing this grunt work for clients has led to them hiring me to do their engineering work for them too. I delivered so well on the grunt work that it opened the door for higher end services.

An important strategy with grunt work is to develop a system of procedures to get it done as efficiently as possible. The system should also have quality control checks to make sure the work is done correctly. Your boss will appreciate this and it will let you free up your thinking time for more challenging work. Having the right procedures in place, means you won't have to reinvent the wheel every time the task comes up.

Take pride in your work. No task your boss assigns is so menial that screwing it up won't matter.

Uncle Mike

Mike Smith ● White Owl Consulting ● 612-555-5550
100 Main St, #310, Minneapolis, MN 55411 ● www.WhiteOwlConsulting.com

From: msmith@whiteowlconsulting.com
Sent: Saturday, September 5, 2009 3:59 PM
To: cdoe@acme-associates.com
Subject: **How to Make a Good First Impression**

Chris,
I can understand you are nervous about your division head coming to the office tomorrow. Take a deep breath. She's a human being too. Just smile and shake her hand. Everything will fall naturally after that.

This is silly, but I learned a lot about making a good first impression from 1993's *My Life*. Bob Jones (played by Michael Keaton) found out he had terminal cancer at the same time his wife found out she was pregnant. Overall it was a downer of a movie, but there was a funny scene that I still remember 15 years later. Bob decides to videotape himself doing things like reading *Green Eggs and Ham* so the child can know his Dad even though he's dead. Part of this videotape series (remember, no You Tube back then) is for when the child is a teenager/young adult. That's where my favorite scene comes in.

Bob goes through the different ways to enter a room and then make an introduction (try to find the clip online if you can). His different walks, saunters, skips, etc. make for a good laugh. He ends up by showing how to walk with a slight forward lean, at a brisk walk (but not jogging), head held high like a military man, with your hand extended as you get near the person. Then you smile, look them in the eye, and introduce yourself - Hi, I'm Bob Jones. Pretty straightforward but the body language is so important. You want to be energetic but not a caricature.

He also goes through how to shake a hand at the end of the routine. No death grips. No dead fish (it's so uncomfortable shaking someone's hand when they don't shake back - they just hold their hand limp). No vigorous pumping of hands up and down or one violent shake down. You should use a controlled, firm but not too firm, grip with two or three shakes.

If you are unsure if you have the handshaking thing down, practice with a friend who is also a professional. These rules are the same for men and women. I think handshaking should be the same for everyone. Guys shouldn't be overly gentle when shaking a woman's hand and women shouldn't overcompensate with the death grip. (I do recognize that other cultures are different – these thoughts apply to Americans).

Be aware that some people may have a hurt hand. I once shook my Uncle Joey's hand and he grimaced. I didn't think I squeezed too hard but he had somehow injured his hand and I aggravated it.

If you are seeing someone you already know you can always go the extra mile; the politician's left hand on the elbow or shoulder in addition to the right handed shake, or the two handed shake. I'm a Midwesterner who was brought up respecting people's personal space so I'm not very good at this style. I am, however comfortable when other people grab my elbow or shoulder. It seems to put me at ease. It's probably something I should work on. Most politicians do it and they are practiced at making a good first impression (it's the follow-up impressions that get them in trouble).

The old axiom is true – you never get a second chance to make a first impression.

Uncle Mike

Mike Smith ● White Owl Consulting ● 612-555-5550
100 Main St, #310, Minneapolis, MN 55411 ● www.WhiteOwlConsulting.com

From: msmith@whiteowlconsulting.com
Sent: Thursday, September 17, 2009 4:12 PM
To: cdoe@acme-associates.com
Subject: **<u>Rules for emailing</u>**

Chris,

Do you miss not being on campus? I always loved the first few weeks of classes (no tests and lots of parties). I get nostalgic this time of year.

This week has been a killer for email. One of my partners sent out an email saying all of the partners needed to meet in an hour to discuss an emergency about one of our big clients. I didn't get the email because I was in the middle of writing a report. Luckily, Paul stopped by on his way to the conference room and grabbed me. Otherwise I would have missed the meeting!

I sent you some thoughts on using outlook, but this episode reminded me there is more I should tell you about email.

Rule one – if something is urgent, don't email. Pick-up the phone and call (would your mom email you if your dad was in a car crash?). You should call if something is a priority and needs to be responded to in an hour or two. Then you can choose to leave a message or hit 0 and try to find out if the person is in the office by talking to a receptionist. Most people are good about returning urgent voicemails within a day.

Rule two - if it is something that isn't urgent, but does need to get through to the person (i.e. a proposal that is due in two days) you should ask for a quick confirmation reply or use the notification alert in your email. If you don't get a response, call the next day. DO NOT call two minutes after sending the email to ask if they received it. People will think you're a pest.

Rule three - put a concise subject in the subject line. I'm not sure why, but some people don't like the subject line. This makes sorting email a pain. You should list the project in a few words along with a teaser of the subject, i.e. Johnson Case - 1/8/09 Meeting Minutes.

Rule four - tell people how you want them to respond. If you are telling people on your team you'll be out of the office for a few days, put FYI in the subject line or in the text so they know they don't have to reply. If you want a specific response, let them know, i.e. please let me know if you can meet on Tuesday at 8 am or Wednesday at 10 am to meet about the Johnson case (be specific instead of generically asking if they are available next week). If you need something specific, email one person and cc anyone else on the email string. If you ask three people a question, odds are no one will respond. Emailing one person forces ownership.

Rule five - be brief. Keep your email to less than a printed page. A paragraph or two is often enough. Email is supposed to be a quick hit medium. Bullet points or numbered lists are also a way for people to quickly digest what you are saying (keep them short though).

Rule six - don't respond to emails that don't need a response. Kind of like the "save a tree, don't print this" message that some people are putting on the bottom of their email. How about a new slogan "save an inbox, only reply when needed."

Emails – be brief, be easy to understand, be done.

Uncle Mike

Mike Smith ● White Owl Consulting ● 612-555-5550
100 Main St, #310, Minneapolis, MN 55411 ● www.WhiteOwlConsulting.com

From: msmith@whiteowlconsulting.com
Sent: Friday, September 18, 2009 10:12 AM
To: cdoe@acme-associates.com
Subject: **Re: Rules for emailing**

Chris,
Big plans for the weekend? Aunt Sara and I are going to the Gopher football game. This is our first time in the U of MN's new stadium. I hear it's fantastic.

I'm glad you like the tips on email. I can't believe you hadn't heard about the delay function for outgoing emails. Hah – your old uncle taught you something about software! Here are a few more thoughts on emails since I have your attention.

Rule seven - send emails outside of normal business hours. This is going to fly in the face of all of those people who want you to have work/life balance. I actually do want you to have some work/life balance, but this is an easy way to gain more points than you deserve. Your boss and client will think you are working really hard after hours for them when in fact you spent ten minutes on an email before bed.

Rule eight - turn off the automatic delivery. Do you remember your first psychology class when they taught about Pavlov's dog? He rang a bell and then gave the dog food. The dog salivated because he saw/smelled the food. Pavlov did this routine to the poor dog a lot. Eventually the dog spit after hearing the bell even before he saw or smelled food because his little brain had been conditioned. Email can be a type of bell for a lot of us. You probably get one or two important emails a week that should be dealt with in four or five hours. Yet every time a message pops up or your computer dings you think you are about to win the lottery. Emails distract you and it takes your brain five to ten minutes to fully get back into the groove of what you were doing before you were rudely interrupted. Do yourself a favor and get your emails only when you ask for them. Better yet, limit yourself to checking the email a few times a day.

Rule nine - use the right tone. Emailing or texting your buddies is a lot different than emailing your boss or client. Be a professional and write respectfully. On the flipside, emails aren't as formal as letters. Rarely should you use "Dear Mr. Smith." "Bob" is a lot more normal with email. The tone of emails is often misinterpreted. Don't be sarcastic, humorous, etc. with your work emails. Assume someone will see your email who won't get it. Your text should stand on its own. The recipient won't see your big grin and know you're joking.

Rule ten - be prompt. Reply to all of your emails within 24 hours. Even if it's just "I got your email. I'll be able to get back to you on Thursday with that info." Warning – if you promise to get back to someone, you need to have a system to remind you to get back to them.

Rule eleven – be careful with the Blackberry. Reading your Blackberry at a stop light and responding as the light turns green can get you in trouble. You should give your work emails more than twenty seconds of attention.

Rule twelve - best for last - assume the world is going to read your email. There are lots of good stories of emails being sent to the wrong people. Lawyers have even done it on cases with catastrophic results. You've probably seen confidentiality clauses on the bottom of some emails. Turns out they don't mean anything in court. If some information could be detrimental, call instead of emailing. If you are worried about someone going to jail, rendezvous on a park bench with trench coats and sunglasses. Don't email!

Think twice before emailing.

Uncle Mike

Mike Smith ● White Owl Consulting ● 612-555-5550
100 Main St, #310, Minneapolis, MN 55411 ● www.WhiteOwlConsulting.com

From: msmith@whiteowlconsulting.com
Sent: Wednesday, October 7, 2009 8:14 PM
To: cdoe@acme-associates.com
Subject: **<u>Taking Minutes</u>**

Chris,

I was wondering when you were going to become the secretary for your team. Congratulations, it only took four months! Most people don't like taking minutes, so bosses often pass this off. Taking the notes usually rolls down to the most junior member at the meeting. It is kind of like hazing for the new guy. At least it will give you something to do at these meetings.

Though most people don't like taking minutes, it's a very important, serious task. Without minutes, it's easy to get different interpretations of what happened. Accurate minutes leave a paper trail everyone can refer to for clarification. Also, meeting minutes are one of the few things you are going to produce at this stage in your career that a lot of people are going to read. Assume the president of Acme is judging you on the quality of the minutes you take.

Start by passing around a sign-in sheet at the meeting to get everyone's name, email address, phone number, and company or department. You'll look more professional if you make up a sign-in sheet ahead of time. It can be as easy as copying the agenda document, deleting the text, inserting a table for people to write in, and changing "Agenda" to "Sign-in". In a pinch, rip a piece of paper off your tablet, write a few headings on it, and pass that around.

You can choose to take minutes on a laptop, but I prefer old fashioned paper and pencil. You can draw arrows and connect ideas faster on paper. My brain listens and takes notes better with pencil and paper, the way I did it in college. I need to concentrate on typing, so I usually miss part of the conversation. Remember, I grew up in the Stone Age before laptops. Do what works for you.

I usually take the electronic version of the one page agenda, put a bunch of spaces in between the agenda items, and print out the expanded (multi-page) agenda. Then I take notes right under the appropriate headings. Leave some blank space at the end to account for new agenda topics.

You can always use a voice recorder too. That will give you a permanent record of the dialogue in addition to your notes.

Now it is time to type up the minutes. No matter how the conversation wandered, I follow the outline everyone agreed to in the agenda. It provides a logical order to the meeting. At the top, under the introduction line item, I type in the attendees. I usually scan in the sign-in sheet and copy/paste it in at the end of the minutes to give everyone a copy. Whenever anyone agreed to do something (or was assigned a task), note an action item in bold, i.e. "**Action Item - Bob** - Email team the atrium drawings by January 18th." It is very important to highlight who is supposed to do what.

HOPEFULLY, you can email the minutes to all of the attendees within 24 hours for their review. You want to get any inaccuracies revised and your best shot is to catch people while the meeting is still fresh in their minds. I copy the action items out of the minutes and put them right in the email, grouped by the responsible person. Some people won't review the minutes because they are too "busy." Copying out the action items is one more way to put people on the hook. It is an easy checklist to go through later too.

If the topic was important enough to meet about, it was important enough to develop thorough and accurate minutes.

Uncle Mike

Mike Smith ● White Owl Consulting ● 612-555-5550
100 Main St, #310, Minneapolis, MN 55411 ● www.WhiteOwlConsulting.com

From: msmith@whiteowlconsulting.com
Sent: Monday, October 12, 2009 10:15 AM
To: cdoe@acme-associates.com
Subject: **You're Not in a Locker-room**

Chris,

I can't believe this, but I just overheard one of our young associates talking about picking up a woman at a bar last weekend. Apparently she was quite attractive and a little drunk. I left before hearing the rest of the story. Trust me. I wasn't eavesdropping. I just happened to be walking by his cube and caught part of his phone conversation. He was talking pretty loud. I am sure people a few cubes away overheard him too.

I am going to assume you know not to talk about personal business at work, especially your drinking and weekend carousing stories. People will overhear your chats, whether your conversations are on the phone or with a guy in the hall.   Here are some other rules for keeping inappropriate, fraternity house behavior out of work:

- Break any cussing habit you have. Swearing makes you sound less intelligent.
- Dump the death metal ringtone on your cell-phone. Pick something innocuous. Better yet, keep your phone on vibrate mode in your pocket.
- Keep your email signature work appropriate. I don't want to see bible verses, catchy quotes or weird clipart. You have a professional image to project.
- Take the keg party pictures off your screensaver.
- Keep the pinup calendar your brother gave you at home.
- Take down the feather boas from around your cube (you aren't working at an internet start-up that promotes that kind of stuff).

Your cube is your home away from home, but think of it as a really boring home. A few pictures of family are ok. A diploma isgood.

Dump the goofball things and look/act like a professional.

Uncle Mike

Mike Smith • White Owl Consulting • 612-555-5550
100 Main St, #310, Minneapolis, MN 55411 • www.WhiteOwlConsulting.com

From: msmith@whiteowlconsulting.com
Sent: Sunday, October 25, 2009 3:59 PM
To: cdoe@acme-associates.com
Subject: **Staying Organized**

Chris,

I don't like raking leaves. My back is already stiffening up, but at least I got it done this weekend. Sometimes I envy your no maintenance, apartment lifestyle.

That's painful that your co-worker lost those documents. Sorry to hear you had to work through the weekend to catch up.

When I was in college your Great Uncle Matt got me a job loading produce trucks for a summer. I worked ten hour nights four to five days a week in the warehouse. I drove around an electric pallet jack, picking the produce for individual grocery stores based on the orders the stores placed earlier that day. I'd stack 20 fifty pound sacks of russet potatoes on my pallet, then 10 sacks of red potatoes, and I'd top it off with sacks of onions. Then I would wrap industrial shrink wrap around the whole thing and put it in the staging area where it would wait to be loaded onto one of the returning semi-trucks. I would cross off the items on the picking slip as I went. Before I pulled away to build another pallet with pineapples, kiwi, strawberries, bananas, etc, I would put an orange sticker on the shrink wrapped pallet and write the name of the receiving grocery store on it. I learned this process on my first day.

Hank, the old timer who trained me in, told me I better cross the picked items off of my picking slip and write the store's name on each pallet while I was doing it so the system was up to date in case I got hit by a forklift and was killed. He wanted to make sure the order could be finished and still go out correctly that night. I quickly learned how replaceable I was!

This is a good lesson for all of us. Follow the filing protocols your company has set up. You never know when you'll be out sick or a funeral will come up. It never fails that while you are gone, the client calls and your boss needs to find something you were working on. Keep your work in order and filed per company policy. If the company filing system is vague, set up your own architecture that you always follow. It will be easier to explain how to find something to a coworker when you are out of the office.

On a personal level, everyone in the office can tell how busy I am by how cluttered my desk is. I'm not one of those guys who works in a rat's nest. I keep my information filed and my desk pretty clear. But when I'm concentrating on a project, files get spread around, reference books are laid open, and drawings are unrolled as I'm cranking away on my computer. It never fails that something gets mixed up when I have two project files open at the same time.

I have learned this lesson repeatedly and I try very hard to keep only one project file open on my desk at a time. I usually clean my desk at the end of the day even if I haven't finished the project. It helps to start the morning with a clean slate.

Keep your files organized and separated so you don't lose anything.

Uncle Mike

Mike Smith ● White Owl Consulting ● 612-555-5550
100 Main St, #310, Minneapolis, MN 55411 ● www.WhiteOwlConsulting.com

From: msmith@whiteowlconsulting.com
Sent: Monday, October 26, 2009 10:42 AM
To: cdoe@acme-associates.com
Subject: **Re: Staying Organized**

Chris,

Yeah – of course I keep an electronic calendar (in Outlook because that's what I've been doing for years, but Google's calendar looks awesome). There are a couple of other tricks I have developed to stay organized. Try out some of these ideas until you settle into your own routine.

To keep my tasks organized, I keep two lists on my desk. One is a "global" to do list that goes through my active projects, potential projects that I should follow-up on later, and long term non-billable projects. This keeps me on track so I don't miss any of the big items. This is my official typed list that I scribble on and retype about every two weeks. I also keep a less official to-do list, completely handwritten, with individual tasks broken down by project for the deadlines I'm working on that week. This list ebbs and flows with tasks being added and crossed off. At the end of the day I make a list of the top three things I need to do the next morning so I can hit the ground running.

I assume just about everyone has a calendar and to-do list of some sort. A slightly less common thing I do is write a phone log. It is just a spiral notebook I keep by my phone so I can track my conversations chronologically. I write the date in the margin by the first call of the day. I try to write the person's name, company and number next to a few words about our call. It's the same process whether I make the call or receive it. It isn't exhaustive, but I find myself paging back occasionally looking for a detail.

I use a bound notebook because I've heard these can be submitted as evidence if I ever get into a lawsuit. Not sure if this is true or not.

Writing things down helps me put them in the back of my brain too. Not that I remember the exact details, but I will remember the call and that I took a note. By accident, I started writing with different colored pencils and pens. Nothing systematic, just whatever I could grab. For some reason I find that the different colors on the phone log help me scan faster when I'm looking back for a certain call.

You can use different electronic programs and paper systems to stay organized. John, one of my mentors, still keeps a paper calendar. He teases me about my computer system, asking me what I'll do if the power dies or the machine blows up.

There are so many tools available now, just about everyone I have ever talked with has a different system for staying organized. Your own system will evolve until you settle into a personal routine that keeps you on target so you don't let anything slip.

Figure out a system to organize your work life that works for you and stick to it religiously.

Uncle Mike

Mike Smith ● White Owl Consulting ● 612-555-5550
100 Main St, #310, Minneapolis, MN 55411 ● www.WhiteOwlConsulting.com

From: msmith@whiteowlconsulting.com
Sent: Tuesday, November 10, 2009 3:39 PM
To: cdoe@acme-associates.com
Subject: **Stop!**

Chris,
Cool down. Find an excuse to get out of the office. Sleep on it and you'll feel differently in the morning.

Be calculating and decisive, but don't make a rash decision.

Uncle Mike

Mike Smith ● White Owl Consulting ● 612-555-5550
100 Main St, #310, Minneapolis, MN 55411 ● www.WhiteOwlConsulting.com

From: msmith@whiteowlconsulting.com
Sent: Friday, November 20, 2009 4:46 PM
To: cdoe@acme-associates.com
Subject: **Procrastinating**

Chris,
I'm putting on my uncle hat to nag for a minute - you can't miss that deadline! You're going to need to work this weekend to get done before Thanksgiving next week.

As I'm sure you know, your grandma was a nurse. She worked in a hospital while she was pregnant with me. About eight months into her pregnancy she was helping a patient who ended up falling on her and she racked her back. My mom's doctor put her on muscle relaxants to help her deal with the pain. No problem, except the muscle relaxants slowed down the birthing process and I was born a month after my due date.

As you can see, I started procrastinating even before I was born, so I feel your pain. In grade school and high school I honed my procrastination skills. Your grandma was always a straight A student and is the type of person who tackles tasks early. As you can imagine, we clashed a lot over my homework as I was growing up. I was lucky, though, and always seemed to be able to work the system and get good grades.

I had straight A's going into finals week of my first semester in college. The physics and calculus covered during most of the semester was a review of stuff I had in high school. I totally blew off studying for finals. I figured I knew it all. I couldn't have been more wrong. I blew the finals so bad I ended up with Cs in physics and calculus. The first C's of my life. Those mediocre grades quickly snapped my procrastination habit.

Dr. Sean McCrea of the University of Konstanz, in Germany, has done interesting studies related to procrastination. He took two study groups and gave them a cash incentive to complete a task. Group 1 was given a lot of information about a specific painting - how it was developed, colors used, brush strokes, etc. Group 2 was given the generic category for the same painting and no other information. Then the folks in the two groups were required to talk about thirteen other paintings. The folks in Group 1 were given specific information and shown how to break the task down into manageable pieces. Group 2 was given little detail. All of their instructions were vague abstractions. It turns out Group 1 significantly outperformed Group 2 even though their motivations (cash) were the same.

As the research team reported in *Psychological Science*, every single person who was given the concrete task and detailed information completed the project on time. Fifty-six percent of the folks given the project in an abstract form didn't complete the project on time. There are a lot of reasons people procrastinate, but it is psychologically powerful when we break a project down into discrete, well-defined tasks. You will also do the work better and faster if you have a good game plan.

So instead of thinking you have to design a building, think about developing a layout for a bathroom. Then break that bathroom down to placing the toilet, vanity, sink, and shower. Design the bathroom and then go onto the next room.

Your boss may or may not be good at helping break down your projects, but it will greatly aid your growth if you develop the habit of breaking your projects into well defined steps that you can work through. It's also easier to get started on something that will take you twenty minutes instead of something that will take you 20 hours.

Break your project into doable tasks so you don't miss that deadline!

Uncle Mike

Mike Smith ● White Owl Consulting ● 612-555-5550
100 Main St, #310, Minneapolis, MN 55411 ● www.WhiteOwlConsulting.com

From: msmith@whiteowlconsulting.com
Sent: Saturday, December 5, 2009 4:39 PM
To: cdoe@acme-associates.com
Subject: **Company Party**

Chris,

That sounds like a great place to have a company party. You should have a very good time. Hopefully your company president doesn't give a long winded talk. Are you going to bring Heather?

I remember the first company party I went to. I started at the same time as Roy, but I didn't know him very well because he worked in a different department. He graduated from Northwestern. I won a few bucks from him when his Wildcats would lose to my Gophers.

I brought Sara to the party (we were married by that point), but Roy came by himself. It was at the old Whitney Hotel. It was a real classy event. A nice sit down dinner and they had an open bar. I am sure I had some cocktails, but I know I didn't keep up with Roy. I think it was his first encounter with an open bar. He ended up getting sick outside the hotel on the sidewalk at the end of the night. I still tease him about this whenever I see him. Even though I tease him in good fun, I bet management didn't appreciate Roy losing control.

Whenever you are with co-workers or clients, you need to drink as slowly as you possibly can. It is also a good idea to mix in a soda pop or water. Avoid the hard alcohol and stick with beer (as long as you won't look out of place). It is easier to nurse a beer without getting tipsy. Never order a girly drink.

The last thing you want is to develop a reputation as a drunk. Remember you are trying to develop an image as a professional. Leave the drinking stories to your college days.

I remember giving this advice to your sister Amy too. Unfortunately, I think this is even more important advice for her. Some guys still have a double standard. They think it is OK for the guys to go out and knock back a few, but they don't think women should drink much. I am not one of those guys, but I know a few.

Lastly, company parties can be a little awkward. You aren't used to socializing with your co-workers and there will be a lot of spouses there. Try to be on your best behavior and be a good conversationalist. Remember that means asking lots of open ended questions and being interested in what they have to say.

Don't get drunk with your co-workers.

Uncle Mike

Mike Smith ● White Owl Consulting ● 612-555-5550
100 Main St, #310, Minneapolis, MN 55411 ● www.WhiteOwlConsulting.com

From: msmith@whiteowlconsulting.com
Sent: Thursday, January 14, 2010 7:52 PM
To: chris@gmail.com
Subject: **Making Your Boss Shine**

Chris,

I'm sorry to hear you aren't getting along with your boss (I'm glad you didn't use your company email, but maybe you should have called me - remember to assume emails will be read by the whole planet someday). You aren't the first person to have a rocky relationship with your boss. Maybe it's the time of year. There is always a letdown at work after the holidays are over.

If your boss truly is a jerk, do not pass go and collect $200, go straight to Bob Sutton's blog. He wrote the book (with the controversial title) *No Asshole Rule*. He has a lot of useful information. His first piece of advice is pretty simple - run! Work as hard as you can to get out of there. Maybe you can get an internal transfer (probably not). You'll probably need to leave the company.

Why not stick it out with a bad boss? The toxic environment is going to rub off on you. As a seasoned veteran, maybe you could make the best of it. Early in your career you should be a sponge learning your craft. A jerk for a boss isn't helping you become the best professional you can be.

OK - I'm going to assume your boss isn't a jerk, he's just a mediocre boss. I have been lucky enough to have good bosses in my career, although some have been better than others. I learned a tremendous amount from each of them and am very grateful for what they taught me. Fortunately for me, each had different strengths I was able to learn from. Try to see the upside in everything you do.

Remember why you have a job. Earn your boss' trust by always delivering on your promises. You will go far in your career if you adopt an underpromise/overdeliver attitude. Always make your deadlines and stay on budget. Don't fall into the temptation of overpromising. Lots of guys back themselves into a corner because they think they'll look great by saying, "I can get you that tomorrow." Sometimes they fail. It's better to say, "I'll get you that in three days." Then if things go perfectly, you can dazzle your client by getting it to them tomorrow. People always like to receive projects early.

Believe it or not, your boss is a human being too. Treat him like one and hopefully things will improve.

Uncle Mike

Mike Smith ● White Owl Consulting ● 612-555-5550
100 Main St, #310, Minneapolis, MN 55411 ● www.WhiteOwlConsulting.com

From: msmith@whiteowlconsulting.com
Sent: Friday, January 15, 2010 1:52 PM
To: chris@gmail.com
Subject: **<u>Making Your Boss Shine continued</u>**

Chris,
I had lunch today with our human resources director (by the way, lunch at Kafe 421 is great). Your situation with your boss came up in the conversation and she had some great ideas on how to get along with a boss - maybe she was sucking up a little bit, since I am technically her boss.

Some more thoughts on working well with your boss -
1. If your boss has a habit of dumping a lot of stuff on you, keep your head down and try to get it done. Sometimes this means burning the midnight candle. If there is no way you can possibly get everything done AND you can't tell what your boss' priorities are, ask for help in prioritizing your tasks. Better to clarify than screw something up.
2. Ask for informal feedback. Don't wait for a formal review. This is a balancing act that is different with every boss. Don't cross over the line. You don't want to be seen as a whiny pest looking for validation every twenty minutes.
3. Be pleasant to be around. It would be inappropriate for you to become close friends, but you should be on good personal terms. Ask your boss about his kid's soccer game that weekend.
4. You'll have a long prosperous career if you are always trying to make your boss' life easier. Keep him in mind when you are prioritizing your tasks. Learn the small things you can do to take things off his plate.
5. Volunteer to help whenever you think you can deliver help.
6. If something is going wrong, let him know ASAP. Just as important, tell him how you are going to fix it. Never bring him a problem without at least one solution.
7. Don't delegate upwards. Take on tasks, don't pass them off to your boss.
8. Solve all of the problems you can without going to your boss. Respect their time.
9. Help your boss with his computer. As someone who didn't grow up with a computer, I know I could use your help.

Work hard to make your boss' life easier.

Uncle Mike

Mike Smith ● White Owl Consulting ● 612-555-5550
100 Main St, #310, Minneapolis, MN 55411 ● www.WhiteOwlConsulting.com

From: msmith@whiteowlconsulting.com
Sent: Saturday, February 6, 2010 7:20 AM
To: Chris@gmail.com
Subject: **Show Me the Money**

Chris,
Congratulations – you're nine months into your career. I think it's time for you to start laying the groundwork to ask for a raise. Don't let your Valentine's Day planning get in the way of doing this.

When I graduated, my first couple of weeks on the job consisted of drawing a parking lot and typing in traffic forecast numbers on figures. I did these things very slowly. It's embarrassing to say this, but I was being overpaid. The truth is that in most professions employees are overpaid for the first two to four years on the job. This is the period when you are "apprenticing." You are learning your craft. Then sometime around year four or five you become competent and self-sufficient. You are paid what you are worth.

Now here is the dirty secret - from about year seven until twenty-five or so most employees are underpaid. This is where the company makes money off of you. It's sad to say, but at the twilight of your career your skills start to erode. A lot of professionals stop learning the new ways of doing things and coast out their career. At this stage they are probably overpaid again. One way to bust the cycle is to become an owner/principal early in that underpaid cycle.

The first critical step in being able to eventually negotiate a raise is being good at your job. You're still learning your craft at this stage in your profession and you're being overpaid. There are probably seasoned technician type folks (i.e. paralegals) who are more productive than you. I don't care. Your learning curve should be progressing quickly and management should see you as a rising star. Someone they want to keep around.

Hopefully the company gives you a decent raise at your one year anniversary. If they do, say thank you very much and then sit tight for a month (you don't want to appear ungrateful). Then it is time to sit down with your boss and tell him that you would like to earn a significant raise at your second anniversary. Lay out your goals and show how you will be helping the company. Don't talk money at this point. Then comes the hard part – follow through on the plan.

Somewhere around your two year anniversary you should go back in and ask for that substantial raise. The company is probably hiring its second batch of graduates after you. Assuming the economy is good, the company is likely offering these folks more than they offered you. It is quite possible they are offering more than you are currently making. Do some online research. Contact the placement office at your alma mater. You may be a little upset to find the new hires are making as much as you. I strongly encouraged your sister Amy to do this, because unfortunately there are still companies out there that pay women less than men.

Now you need to make a gut decision. How much should you ask for? Maybe a 20% raise? Make sure you have some rationale on why you are asking for that much. You'll need to prove that you are bringing sufficient value to the company so that your raise is justified. Part of this is asking for more responsibility.

Caveat - if the company or economy is doing poorly, hold tight and be grateful you have a pay check.

Start laying the groundwork to get that first big raise.

Uncle Mike

Mike Smith ● White Owl Consulting ● 612-555-5550
100 Main St, #310, Minneapolis, MN 55411 ● www.WhiteOwlConsulting.com

From: msmith@whiteowlconsulting.com
Sent: Sunday, February 21, 2010 4:01 PM
To: Chris@gmail.com
Subject: **Re: Insider Info**

Chris,
Sorry to hear you and Heather broke up the day before Valentine's Day. That's harsh.

It was nice of your boss to take you to the game yesterday. You are right to feel a little funny though. It's strange the tickets ended up being to one of your competitor's box suite - even if his college buddy is a VP over there. It's even stranger that the VP seemed to be asking you a lot of questions about your projects.

Maybe everything is on the up and up, but I always go back to the sniff test when thinking about ethics. If something smells like trash, it is trash. Keep your guard up. Never give out inside information to competitors or even clients for that matter. You are too early in your career to know what is appropriate and what isn't appropriate. Err on the side of caution.

I am not saying don't help people in your network, just don't share information about your company. Your role in your network is to be a matchmaker between two entities. Priority one is to match up your company with another one. Priority two is to match up two other companies after you determine your company doesn't have a role to play.

Now there is a much stickier issue here – is your boss feeding intelligence to the competition? I always assume innocent until proven guilty. Let's assume he is just hanging out with friends and not doing any harm to Acme. BUT – pay attention. If you see a pattern, document it and bring your concerns higher up the chain of command. If that happens, we need to talk through your strategy because this is an extremely delicate situation. You need to be straightforward and well documented, but you can't be too strong.

In the meantime, I think sunlight is the best disinfectant. Hopefully you will be in an informal setting with your boss and his boss in the next week. Casually bring up that you had a great time at the game and it was nice to meet all of those folks from the competing firm. Innocently say you didn't realize you were on such good terms with them. Then drop it.

You have put your boss and his boss on notice without putting your neck on the line. If your boss berates you later, it is a strong sign he is doing something inappropriate.

In any event, know what Acme's policies are regarding presents, tickets, etc. There isn't a good reason for you to break the company policies.

Use your gut. If something seems inappropriate, it probably is.

Uncle Mike

Mike Smith ● White Owl Consulting ● 612-555-5550
100 Main St, #310, Minneapolis, MN 55411 ● www.WhiteOwlConsulting.com

From: msmith@whiteowlconsulting.com
Sent: Thursday, February 25, 2010 9:48 PM
To: cdoe@acme-associates.com
Subject: **Don't Be the Bottleneck**

Chris,
Wow is it cold! Your Aunt Sara wants to move to Arizona, but she always seems to be cold.

Cool project. It's encouraging to hear your boss is starting to give you some real work. In engineering school I took a class on project management. It was a nice departure from the design classes I had been taking. We learned the basics of gantt charts and a few concepts about management.

Gantt charts are fancy bar charts that help people map out the steps in a process. They are a tool that helps you think through your schedule. Most importantly, they help you identify the critical path for getting the project done by linking the steps that have to be done one after the other (the things you can't do simultaneously). Gantt charts used to be time consuming to make, but were necessary for large projects like building a dam. Now programs such as Microsoft Project make it easy to prepare these charts.

I imagine you aren't working in a vacuum but are on a team doing your part to help complete the big project. You have a piece of it, but aren't in charge. Here is the key to being a good team member - DON'T BE THE BOTTLENECK.

What do I mean? Do your work on time so you aren't holding up anyone else from getting their work done. If you are on the hot seat and somebody is waiting for your information, work as hard and as fast as you can to get off the hot seat. Think about the bottleneck like a hot potato. If you catch the hot potato, pass it to the next guy as fast as possible. Two examples of how this works on my projects.

One - I prepare traffic studies as a component to large environmental review documents. These documents look at everything from noise impacts to potential archeological issues. I'm responsible for one of the thirty or so things that go into the overall environmental study. My job is to make sure my traffic study is not the thirtieth thing to get done. I don't want to hold up a developer's approval process. So I find out the team's deadline and work to beat it. Hopefully I beat the deadline by weeks. Shooting for weeks early allows me to still meet the deadline if everything goes wrong on my end.

Two - A little simpler scenario. I recommend a design for adding a turn lane as part of one of my traffic studies. The civil engineer who is doing the road design leaves me a voicemail to double check how long that turn lane should be. I call him back as soon as I get the message. I don't want to slow up his design process and screw up our client's schedule.

Key to not being the bottleneck is having all of the information and data you need at your fingertips. Always spend fifteen minutes when you are assigned a new task to think through the data and information you will need. If you don't have it, start the process for getting it immediately. It will probably take you five minutes to write the email or make the phone call, but you are going to be in a bind if you haven't made the request and you realize your deadline is tomorrow.

Always try to be ahead of the curve.

Uncle Mike

Mike Smith ● White Owl Consulting ● 612-555-5550
100 Main St, #310, Minneapolis, MN 55411 ● www.WhiteOwlConsulting.com

From: msmith@whiteowlconsulting.com
Sent: Monday, March 8, 2010 10:49 AM
To: cdoe@acme-associates.com
Subject: **Joe the Complainer**

Chris,

There was a guy named "Joe" at one of the places I worked who sounds a lot like your co-worker. He liked to walk around with a cup of coffee and stop in people's doorways. He'd lean against the office doorway or cube entrance trapping his prey. Once there, it took twenty to thirty minutes to get Joe to move on. Between the official coffee breaks he took, these wanderings, and his heavy meeting schedule, I think he was productive for about eight and a half minutes a day. He was like a character out of the movie *Office Space*. Joe could drain the productivity out of your whole morning if you let him.

Every office has a Joe or two. He is the guy who is never happy (except when he is letting you know why he is unhappy). An agitator - hey we should form a union so the man can't beat on us. Look in the mirror and make sure you aren't like Joe. If you are becoming a Joe, force yourself to smile and work to break this bad habit. Never complain to your co-workers or your boss (you can put a picture of his face on your punching bag at home if you need to). Just keep your head down and work.

After you make sure you aren't Joe, figure out the folks in your office who are the complainers. Now stay away from them. Attitudes are as contagious as the flu. Gravitate towards people who are upbeat. The people who look at problems as opportunities. Over time, you will notice you assimilate to your environment. You develop expectations consistent with your friends, significant other, and the co-workers you hang out with. Choose wisely.

Now, how are you going to deal with Joe at the office? I hope I am a nice guy and I think you are. We want to be on good terms with Joe. I believe we should be pleasant with everyone we meet (except perhaps the attorney Ivan the Jerk). Make two minutes of small talk in the hallway and then excuse yourself - you need to get back to the grind. Don't become a confidant of Joe's or he'll feel more compelled to stop at your cube every time the man beats down on him. When you notice Joe walking by your cube, concentrate on your computer or your desk. Don't make eye contact. Don't acknowledge that he is nearby. Be so into your work that you don't give him an easy opening to start a conversation.

Joe may cough or actually say something to interrupt you. You can't give in to Joe, but you are his co-worker. He may actually have something work related to go over. Be polite, ask him what you can do to help him. Quickly get to the point, make a few notes of your conversation. Then tell Joe you are in the middle of a project with a big deadline and you need to get back to it.

Hopefully you don't have to be too forceful. Joe may have real issues in his personal or professional life.

You don't need to be rude, but you should protect your work turf. You need to be productive. Be thankful you're not a manager yet. If you were Joe's boss, you'd have to work more diligently with him on a personal and work level.

Don't let Joe the Complainer zap your productivity!

Uncle Mike

p.s. Any March Madness picks for me? I never do well in the NCAA basketball pool.

Mike Smith • White Owl Consulting • 612-555-5550
100 Main St, #310, Minneapolis, MN 55411 • www.WhiteOwlConsulting.com

From: msmith@whiteowlconsulting.com
Sent: Friday, March 19, 2010 4:13 PM
To: cdoe@acme-associates.com
Subject: **Dr. Scribbles**

Chris,
Emma was sick and I took her to the doctor. Not a big deal, but she needs some antibiotics. Why is it so hard to read a doctor's signature on a prescription? It's laughable to think a doctor's signature is a requirement to get drugs. How on earth does the pharmacist know the doctor signed it? My three year old can scribble on par with some of the signatures I have seen.

If something is worth signing, it seems to me that it should be signed with a name that can be read. If your name is so long that the extra fourteen seconds it takes to legibly write your name are destroying your productivity, use your first and middle name initials with your last name. Your signature should be a manner of pride. It says a lot about you.

If you are a scribbler, take some time to test out new signatures. Come up with something that could be understood if your name wasn't typed out underneath it. If you want something big and bold, figure out a John Hancock. (Would we remember John Hancock 200+ years later if it wasn't for his legible signature?)

My signature was straight out of my cursive writing lessons until I was 22. I decided it looked too childish when I got into the working world. I tried two pages of different ways I could sign my name and settled on a signature that's a combination of letters from my Grandma's signature, my Dad's signature, and my third grade penmanship class. In my opinion, it is now both professional and legible.

Take pride in your signature.

Uncle Mike

Mike Smith • White Owl Consulting • 612-555-5550
100 Main St, #310, Minneapolis, MN 55411 • www.WhiteOwlConsulting.com

From: msmith@whiteowlconsulting.com
Sent: Thursday, April 8, 2010 7:28 PM
To: cdoe@acme-associates.com
Subject: **Focus**

Chris,

It finally hit sixty degrees! About ten students showed up to my class at the U. I think I saw the rest of my students playing frisbee as I walked through campus. I always have to remind myself to stay the course this time of year. I was one of those frisbee players in college and the urge to "skip class" still plagues me when the weather finally turns nice.

George has been a great mentor for me throughout my career. He was president of a 120 person consulting engineering firm when I interviewed with him my senior year of college. He tried to get me to take a job in one of his company's rural offices, but I declined. I was engaged to Sara and she was starting graduate school in Minneapolis that fall. I couldn't imagine moving away from her. Since then I have managed to grab breakfast with George at least once a year.

At one of our breakfast meetings early in my career, I asked him how he rose to be president of his firm. He talked about a very big project he landed midway in his career and how he worked very long hours to get that project successfully delivered. That project in turn helped him become a rainmaker (a person who brings in work – i.e. makes rain) as well as a good manager. He thought the Board of Directors really took notice of him then. But then George said something that still sticks with me, even though it was a tangent. The gist of the tangent was he thinks he gets more done during a workday than most of the other people in the office.

I asked him how he gets more done and he didn't have any profound insight. He doesn't spend a lot of time at the coffee pot, he tackles the important stuff (not always the urgent stuff, but the stuff that will matter years later) on his to-do list first, he keeps his head down and stays focused. This doesn't mean he rushes through his to-do list.

Oops – I have to run. I'll send you my personal plan for staying focused tomorrow.

As John Wooden, the retired UCLA basketball coach says – "be quick, but don't hurry."

Uncle Mike

Mike Smith • White Owl Consulting • 612-555-5550
100 Main St, #310, Minneapolis, MN 55411 • www.WhiteOwlConsulting.com

From: msmith@whiteowlconsulting.com
Sent: Friday, April 9, 2010 10:18 AM
To: cdoe@acme-associates.com
Subject: **Focus continued**

Chris,

As promised, here is my recipe for staying focused:

1. Five minutes before you are ready to leave at the end of the work day, tidy up your desk and update your to-do list. Flag the first three things you are going to do in the morning.

2. When you get in the next morning, dive into the first thing on your to-do list. After you have accomplished your first task (assuming it takes less than an hour), check your voicemail and email. Knocking off your first task before getting sucked into other people's priorities will set you up for a productive day.

3. When you get a new project, outline the tasks you'll need to do to get it done. Immediately start working on getting the things or data you will need from other people. You can always let the information sit for a few weeks, but you might not be able to get the info when you need it if you wait until the last minute. Think ahead so you avoid road blocks in your project.

4. Check your email again mid-morning and mid-afternoon (easier said than done). This means ignoring the Blackberry most of the day. Email is amazingly distracting.

5. Early in your career you probably have the luxury of not being interrupted very often. Savor this and try to work in 60 minute blocks. After an hour or so, take a few minutes break to recharge. It is easier to run a race when you know where the finish line is. Schedule sixty minute races for yourself.

6. It's fine to talk about last night's game at the watercooler. Those relationships may help you later. Just don't be the guy who stands there for half an hour.

7. When you have something important to think about or review, get out of the office and turn off your iPhone. When I do my final review of reports and designs, I pack up and head to a coffee shop. I get a treat, spread out, and spend a few hours. I studied at coffee shops in college, so my brain is conditioned to focus in that environment. Figure out your own hideout where you can go when you need to really focus on something. Get away from the phone, your email, Joe the Complainer, and your boss. Do these

important tasks when your brain works best – for me this is first thing in the morning.

Find your focus and work to keep it in spite of life's distractions.

Uncle Mike

p.s. Do you have your taxes done yet? April 15th is less than a week away.

Mike Smith ● White Owl Consulting ● 612-555-5550
100 Main St, #310, Minneapolis, MN 55411 ● www.WhiteOwlConsulting.com

From: msmith@whiteowlconsulting.com
Sent: Sunday, May 2, 2010 4:26 PM
To: cdoe@acme-associates.com
Subject: **Support Staff**

Chris,
Do you have plans next Saturday? I could use some help putting in the dock at the cabin. Can you bring a couple of your buddies? As usual, I pay in beer.

Don't get mad at Jenny. She is there to help you and she still knows more than you do. Plus, she could make your life tough if she wants to. You need her on your side.

I have an administrative person who is my right hand in the office. The last time I had to do layoffs, she helped me decide who to let go. I trust her judgment and assume if people are jerks to her, they probably aren't representing our company well.

The second day in my internship at the City of St. Paul my boss told me to go over to Aaron and see what he had going on. Aaron is a technician who drafts the plans for traffic signals in the city. He also does a lot of inspecting on traffic signal and lighting projects. So Aaron had me hop in the car with him and we did some inspections. During my six month internship I spent more time with Aaron than anyone else. He taught me most of his job. I learned how things really work with traffic signals.

I had a similar experience after graduation when I started at Bloomfield. The technician/draftsman on our team was Lee. He taught me how to use AutoCAD and the basics of traffic signal design. If it wasn't for Aaron and Lee, I would know very little about traffic signals. Now I make my living designing them.

A lot of knowledge resides in the support staff around you. Respect them. They probably know the basics of your job better than you do. Paralegals can do everything a freshly minted lawyer can, just faster. The receptionist at the front desk knows the filing system inside and out. Ask them for help and say thank you. They are very important to you, especially in your first year on the job.

Don't be the jerk who talks down to support staff – you need them more than they need you.

Uncle Mike

Mike Smith ● White Owl Consulting ● 612-555-5550
100 Main St, #310, Minneapolis, MN 55411 ● www.WhiteOwlConsulting.com

From: msmith@whiteowlconsulting.com
Sent: Wednesday, May 19, 2010 3:46 PM
To: cdoe@acme-associates.com
Subject: **Lowrider**

Chris,
Your sister tells me you are starting to look for a new car. I know a young engineer who drives a very expensive car and I don't think it's the best choice for him at this point in his career. Here are a few things I think you should consider before you drive off the lot –

When I started my first civil engineering job, all the partners in the firm drove company-owned Buick Park Avenues. Stodgy cars. Respectable, reliable, but not flashy. Shortly after I joined the firm my family was at a restaurant celebrating my parent's 25th wedding anniversary. Harry, one of the firm's partners, was dining there with his wife. We left at the same time and I saw him drive off in a brand new, top of the line Cadillac.

The next day I asked my boss why Harry didn't drive the Cadi to work. He told me the Cadillac was Harry's weekend car. Harry had more than enough money to afford the Cadillac and he liked driving it. But the partners had decided neither the employees nor the clients should see them driving expensive cars. The firm had made the conscious decision not to appear to be living the high life. The partners tied their company brand to Buick's brand – respectable, reliable, and not flashy.

One of the engineers at the firm who wasn't a partner drove a Cadillac every day. There was more gossip than you would think about that car. The gossip was that the partners thought he was a show-off. I don't know if the Cadillac was necessarily a contributor, but he was never made a partner.

My good friend Terry ran a Dairy Queen in college. The lady who owned the DQ drove a twenty year old rust bucket of a station wagon. Terry used to talk about that car. This lady had come from a wealthy family, owned a fair amount of property and probably was independently wealthy herself. But most of her tenants had no idea she had money. She was a shrewd negotiator who was always looking for an angle. The station wagon was part of her workday image.

What kind of car should you get? What kind of image should you be sending to your co-workers and your clients? Does your car fit that image? Think about it and don't rationalize an emotional decision. And when you get it, keep it clean in case you need to drive co-workers or clients to a meeting.

Your car is part of your professional image. Make a logical choice.

Uncle Mike

p.s. Remember new cars drop a lot in value the second you drive away from the dealership. A lot of people think of a car as an asset. It is really a depreciating asset - the vast majority of cars keep going down in value (they aren't an investment). You should consider buying a used car (I like one year old cars with about 15,000 miles on them. They are still under warranty and should be in great condition.). Keep your car in good condition and drive it for at least five years. Save your money.

Mike Smith • White Owl Consulting • 612-555-5550
100 Main St, #310, Minneapolis, MN 55411 • www.WhiteOwlConsulting.com

From: msmith@whiteowlconsulting.com
Sent: Tuesday, June 8, 2010 7:15 AM
To: cdoe@acme-associates.com
Subject: **Goal Setting**

Chris,

Congratulations on surviving your first year on the job! I bet you're ready to take the summer off. I think you should spend an hour or two with a cup of coffee (or a beer) this weekend thinking about where you are going. Having goals is important.

The business school at Harvard started a little study with MBA students in 1979. They asked the graduates if they had written goals. 3% of them had written goals and plans. Ten years later the professor went back and interviewed the MBAs. He found that the 3% with the written goals were earning ten times the amount of money as their non-goal writing peers. WOW!

Too bad this is an often repeated urban legend. Google this story and you'll see thousands of hits about it. It has even been written about in books. There is a similar story about Yale students of 1953. Yale University issued an official statement saying it wasn't true. *Fast Company* magazine did an article debunking the myth.

Lucky for us, Dr. Gail Matthews at Dominican University in California researched the urban myth. She concluded that such studies never existed and then decided to do her own experiment on goals. She broke 149 students into five groups who then worked on setting goals to be accomplished over four weeks:
- Group 1 thought about their goals.
- Group 2 wrote down their goals.
- Group 3 wrote their goals and developed action commitments.
- Group 4 wrote their goals, developed action commitments and sent their written document to a supportive friend.
- Group 5 wrote their goals, developed action commitments, sent this written document to a supportive friend and also sent their supportive friend a weekly progress report.

Achievement of their goals was measured on a scale from 1 to 8 with 8 being best. The groups with the above strategies scored:

- Group 1 - 4.28
- Group 2 - 6.08
- Group 3 - 5.08
- Group 4 - 6.41
- Group 5 - 7.60

Thanks to Dr. Matthews work we have advanced the power of goal setting from urban legend to solid academic fact. The act of writing down your goals will increase your odds of achieving them by about 50%. Going all of the way to writing down your goals, developing an action plan, and being accountable to a friend on a weekly basis will nearly double your odds of achieving your goals.

Even though the study was on short term goals, my personal experience with using the last method for long term goal setting makes me think it works for long term goals too. I hope you'll develop long term (5 to 10 year) goals. Then break them up into one year goals that you can break down even farther into an action plan that you can work on weekly. Writing them down is a huge step forward. Sharing your weekly progress with your boss or a friend will push you even further.

Set goals and make yourself accountable for reaching them.

Uncle Mike

Mike Smith • White Owl Consulting • 612-555-5550
100 Main St, #310, Minneapolis, MN 55411 • www.WhiteOwlConsulting.com

From: msmith@whiteowlconsulting.com
Sent: Tuesday, June 15, 2010 4:52 PM
To: cdoe@acme-associates.com
Subject: **Time to Ask for Raise**

Chris,
A few months ago, your boss agreed to your plan for a raise. Don't forget to check in with him since you just had your one year anniversary.

Make sure you are on track for that significant raise.

Uncle Mike

Mike Smith • White Owl Consulting • 612-555-5550
100 Main St, #310, Minneapolis, MN 55411 • www.WhiteOwlConsulting.com

From: msmith@whiteowlconsulting.com
Sent: Monday, June 28, 2010 10:01 AM
To: cdoe@acme-associates.com
Subject: **Time to be a Joiner**

Chris,
It was great to see you this weekend. I am glad we caught some fish. Your dad is a good guide. One thing I thought of as I was driving home – it's time for you to join a professional society.

My career path trajectory wasn't set for me until I went to a professional society meeting a month before I graduated. The economy was tight and I was still looking for a job. I sat at a table with seven other people, including a guy named Will who worked at Bloomfield and Associates. He mentioned they were thinking about hiring a civil engineer fresh out of college for their traffic engineering department. I was pretty dumb back then (some things don't change much), but I was smart enough to call him later that week. After a few months of being persistent with my follow-up, I was offered that traffic engineering job at Bloomfield.

My boss at Bloomfield, John, has been very involved with the professional society. He even worked his way up to the international board of directors. He pushed me to stay involved with the society's local section and be active on committees.

He was smart enough to insist that I work on a committee and then work my way up to becoming a committee chair. That is the best way to get to know people and build a level of trust outside of your office. You will learn something too.

I agreed to be the section's newsletter co-editor (producing a worthwhile quarterly newsletter is a lot of work). That started getting my name out there in the traffic engineering community. I rose up through the section's board until I was president. After eight years of involvement, I knew just about every traffic engineer in the state. Not only was it good for my professional development, but I have made a lot of great friends.

This became the springboard for starting my own firm. I started doing subconsultant work for my friends who work at the local consulting firms. They eventually started referring business to me when they had conflict of interest issues. I wouldn't have known these people if I hadn't been involved with my professional society.

Even if your company won't pay for it and you have to put in your own time, I strongly recommend you get involved with a professional society, trade association, chamber of commerce, rotary club, etc. where you can start networking. As a professional, you need to know people if you are going to advance in your career. Even if you don't make stellar business contacts, you'll learn how to interact with people who aren't your direct co-workers. Meeting people at professional society meetings and sub-committees is the best way you can start. If transportation engineers have had a professional society since 1930, your profession must have one too.

The old cliché has stuck around because it is true – it isn't always what you know, but who you know.

Uncle Mike

Mike Smith • White Owl Consulting • 612-555-5550
100 Main St, #310, Minneapolis, MN 55411 • www.WhiteOwlConsulting.com

From: msmith@whiteowlconsulting.com
Sent: Friday, July 2, 2010 7:49 AM
To: cdoe@acme-associates.com
Subject: **Reading, Writing, and Arithmetic**

Chris,
So your boss just got back from hearing a management guru and he thinks he should help you work on your weaknesses. Tread lightly.

Ever since my dad and grandpa taught me to play cribbage, I have been able to visualize numbers and manipulate them in my head - like I was twisting a Rubik's cube. Cribbage taught me to combine numbers in different ways and to see patterns. I am still good with numbers in my head. Understanding numbers is one of my strengths. It isn't very shocking that I ended up as an engineer. I could have become an accountant too.

For some reason though, I don't have a great memory. I would try, but I was weaker in subjects like history and biology where there was a lot of memorization. I tried to stay away from memorization based classes in college. I originally got on the engineering track because I didn't want to take a foreign language as was required in the college of liberal arts. Calculus instead of Spanish!

A lot of people say you should work on your weaknesses. I strongly disagree. There are some basic skills you need in order to be a member of our society; reading, writing, and arithmetic being among them. I hope you learned these basics before you got to high school. I am not arguing against being able to read if you are great at math. But after junior high you should focus on what you are good at. The personality and brain have developed enough by that point so a person can start to figure out their areas of strengths and weaknesses. Think about the people we admire. If Einstein was bad at painting would you have told him to devote his life to it and skip the physics stuff? Would you tell Hemingway to put away the typewriter and become an accountant for the sake of balance? The idea of devoting a lot of time to your weaknesses is absurd.

Being a professional is all about being a specialist. You need to focus your knowledge by working on your strengths. If for some reason, you picked a profession that is a weakness - start over because you are going to be a flop. Even if you become average through a lifetime of working against yourself, you aren't going to have fun.

I hope you'll pattern yourself after your Aunt Louise. She did chemistry research that was published as an undergraduate and she was getting great grades in her chemistry/pre-med track. Louise thought she wanted to be a pediatrician because she loves working with kids. Midway through college she realized medical school wasn't the best fit for her and she switched to education. She is an amazingly good elementary school teacher. She honed in on her strengths/passions and I think she is happier than if she were a doctor.

Swim with the current instead of against it – improve your strengths instead of your weaknesses.

Uncle Mike

p.s. Are you going to the 4th of July family picnic?

Mike Smith ● White Owl Consulting ● 612-555-5550
100 Main St, #310, Minneapolis, MN 55411 ● www.WhiteOwlConsulting.com

From: msmith@whiteowlconsulting.com
Sent: Tuesday, July 20, 2010 8:18 PM
To: cdoe@acme-associates.com
Subject: **<u>Meeting Etiquette</u>**

Chris,
Boring meetings suck, but unfortunately you are going to have to get used to them. The company is paying you a good wage. Attending boring meetings is part of the way you earn your paycheck. I'm glad to hear you didn't fall asleep. That would have been embarrassing (like the time I fell asleep in an auditorium sized freshman history class and started snoring).

Unfortunately, many organizations confuse activity with progress. The bigger the company or agency, the worse it gets. At this early stage in your career, you don't have much ability to say "no" to attending meetings (more power to you if you can). In fact, it is probably so much a part the culture, you'll need to attend meetings in order to be promoted.

A few years ago I was in the audience at a county board meeting waiting for my client's project to be discussed. The engineers and developers talking before me were saying some really stupid things. My client was whispering to me in the back and made a wise crack. I had a very inappropriate chuckle. No real damage was done, but I felt and looked very disrespectful. Not at all professional.

The first rule I want you to follow when you are in a meeting comes from Abraham Lincoln who said, "Better to remain silent and be thought a fool than to speak out and remove all doubt." This has been a hard lesson for me and is a hard lesson for most professionals who want to prove they are experts. Not only shouldn't you chuckle, but in general you should talk less. Stick to your expertise and the things you know. Don't throw in a tangent or speculate on things that are outside of your realm. There comes a time when you should speak up, but you need to know what you are talking about to pull it off.

The second rule is based on watching Barack Obama in debates. He is very calm and attentive. He exudes confidence with his body language. Don't tap your pencil. Don't slouch in your chair. Don't grunt or laugh. Fake being attentive even if you are bored out of your mind. This also means never checking your Blackberry.

The third and last rule is to take notes, even if they are brief scribbling. I learned this in college. It'll help you pay attention to the discussion and it's hard to fall asleep if you are writing. But don't just doodle. Someone in the room may see your doodlings and be offended because you aren't paying attention.

No matter how boring the meeting, you are being paid to be there. Give them your attention.

Uncle Mike

Mike Smith ● White Owl Consulting ● 612-555-5550
100 Main St, #310, Minneapolis, MN 55411 ● www.WhiteOwlConsulting.com

From: msmith@whiteowlconsulting.com
Sent: Friday, August 6, 2010 4:23 PM
To: cdoe@acme-associates.com
Subject: **Re: My Boss Was Fired**

Chris,
Wow! After what you have told me about him, I am not surprised he was
let go.   It sounds like your whole division is going through a re-
organization. This is a great opportunity for you to expand your role in
the company. Try not to get caught up in the hallway gossip. Now is a
bad time to get distracted from your work. Keep doing what you have
been doing.   You must have made a positive impression on upper
management. Be happy you survived the layoffs. Call me if you start to
feel any survivor's guilt and we can go out for a beer. Celebrate having a
job and watch the Twins tonight. I think they are going to win the
pennant this year.

Do you have a new boss yet?   Do you know where you and your
department fit into the org chart yet? There will be opportunities, but
there will also be some landmines to avoid.

In this situation you are going to need to educate your boss about who
you are – how much experience you have, what your accomplishments
are, and what you are capable of. This is more difficult than starting a
new job because your whole division is in a state of turmoil.

Make a bullet point list to go over with your new boss.
- Your accomplishments so far on the job
- What projects you are currently working (include a status
  summary for each project)
- Lay out your current responsibilities and prioritize them from
  your vantage point
- General thoughts on how the division used to work (pros that
  should potentially be kept and cons that should be discontinued)
- Any urgent items that have to be dealt with in the next week
- The one year plan you developed as part of your planned raise
  request

Try to get your new boss out of the office to go through your list. Going
out to lunch or grabbing coffee one on one would be good. You want to

be in a setting where you feel you can be honest and straightforward. You have two goals with this meeting – (1) try to help your new boss in the transition and (2) make a strong first impression.

We'll assume you are getting a great boss. Start laying the groundwork for becoming a trusted employee. Don't be pushy and don't be overwhelming. Put yourself in her shoes and try to give her the information you would want if the roles were reversed. Hopefully, she'll appreciate going over your list. You want to be efficient, not needy. Remember, she's settling into a new role and will need some time to get a feel for your department. Until she tells you differently, keep plugging away on your projects. Don't forget to routinely ask her how you can help.

Re-organizations are opportunities to become even more valuable to the company.

Uncle Mike

Mike Smith ● White Owl Consulting ● 612-555-5550
100 Main St, #310, Minneapolis, MN 55411 ● www.WhiteOwlConsulting.com

From: msmith@whiteowlconsulting.com
Sent: Monday, August 30, 2010 4:39 PM
To: cdoe@acme-associates.com
Subject: **Silence is Golden**

Chris,
I went to Target Field yesterday to watch the Twins lose. The new stadium is great, too bad the Twins are slumping. There goes the pennant.

Sorry to hear you put your foot in your mouth. You're hardly alone.

I was sitting next to my client and some of his consultants at a city council public hearing a while ago. My client's architect was presenting the development plan to the city council as part of the city's approval process. The architect was about ten minutes through his thirty minute presentation when the mayor politely stopped him. The mayor took a quick straw poll and it looked like the council was going to approve the whole plan on the spot. Then the architect interrupted them and said he had this great 3-D simulation of the building that he wanted to go through. It was clear he spent a lot of effort on this model and was proud of it. The mayor grumbled a little, but the architect pushed.

A few minutes into walking through the building simulation one of the council members started asking questions about what they were seeing. The council members started to see details they didn't like. The architect was on his heels like he was being pummeled by the Teenage Mutant Ninja Turtles (one of the old school Nintendo games I was addicted to in high school). My client, the developer, jumped up and forced the architect to sit down. He got the city council to agree to table the application so the team could regroup and come back in a month.

There is an important lesson here that most salespeople learn early in their career. If someone agrees to buy, you should smile, say thank you, shut up, and leave with the signed order as fast as you can. As professionals, we are wrapped up in our persona as an expert. We spend a lot of time in college getting a difficult degree and we like to show we are experts, especially when we (like the poor architect) have prepared so hard to say more than is necessary. It's hard to deal with silence. A pause in the conversation is tough to sit through. But as a true professional you need to get comfortable with silence.

Minimize the opportunities to put your foot in your mouth.

Uncle Mike

Mike Smith ● White Owl Consulting ● 612-555-5550
100 Main St, #310, Minneapolis, MN 55411 ● www.WhiteOwlConsulting.com

From: msmith@whiteowlconsulting.com
Sent: Tuesday, August 31, 2010 9:18 PM
To: cdoe@acme-associates.com
Subject: **Speak up**

Chris,

I shot you an email yesterday about staying quiet. Then I remembered something I read about "leaders" and I dug it out this evening. I still think part of maturing as a professional is learning when to be quiet, but research shows you should be selective about keeping quiet. On top of being quiet you need to know when to speak up.

Cameron Anderson and Gavin Kilduff did a research study at the University of California – Berkley to determine perceived leadership (http://repositories.cdlib.org/iir/iirwps/iirwps-159-07). They put people into teams (all male or all female so there wouldn't be any gender bias) and gave them the task of developing an imaginary, non-profit environmental organization. Other researchers determined the best plan and the winning team got $400.

Kilduff, Anderson, and the outside researchers rated the participants for their leadership skills. The quietest team members were ranked by the researchers as the most "conventional and uncreative." The team members who spoke the most were rated highly and seen as "dependable and self-disciplined."

The same experiment was done again, but with the task of solving math and logic problems from the GMAT instead of developing the framework for a non-profit. This was an objective test versus the subjective test of coming up with the best non-profit. Again, those who spoke most were seen as the leaders and those who were quiet weren't highly rated.

Here's the rub, there was a corollary between talking up and being perceived as a leader but the actual performance on the GMAT problems found no corollaries between speaking up and correctly leading the team. So real leadership has nothing to do with speaking up, but speaking up has everything to do with being perceived as a leader.

True professionals need to be perceived as real leaders. The ideal situation is to speak up AND be a good leader. I want you to learn the lesson of shutting up once someone has "bought what you are selling," but the takeaway of this research is that you need to be a talker in group situations. Holding your tongue will likely sabotage your career. People might think you have nothing to add.

To be perceived as an intelligent, leading professional you'll need to speak up. Don't be a wallflower.

Uncle Mike

Mike Smith • White Owl Consulting • 612-555-5550
100 Main St, #310, Minneapolis, MN 55411 • www.WhiteOwlConsulting.com

From: msmith@whiteowlconsulting.com
Sent: Monday, September 6, 2010 3:48 PM
To: cdoe@acme-associates.com
Subject: **Re: Funny Joke**

Chris,
1. That was a good joke.
2. Don't send these types of things during work or from your work email. While you're at it, make sure you don't send jokes to your co-workers. Don't forward chain letters (Microsoft isn't going to send you any money if you forward the email on to ten people). Don't get sucked into urban myths. Don't reply to any barristers from Nigeria.

Work email is for work. Don't forward inappropriate stuff.

Uncle Mike

p.s. You know I like good jokes. Send them to me after hours from your gmail account.

Mike Smith • White Owl Consulting • 612-555-5550
100 Main St, #310, Minneapolis, MN 55411 • www.WhiteOwlConsulting.com

From: msmith@whiteowlconsulting.com
Sent: Tuesday, September 14, 2010 8:58 PM
To: cdoe@acme-associates.com
Subject: **Problem Solving via the Memo**

Chris,

That's a tough one. I'm not sure what you should do. The first time I had
to make a real decision I ran into my boss' office and asked him what he
thought. I don't even remember what the issue was, but I'm sure I
thought it was really important. John asked me what I thought, to which
I responded by stumbling and stammering. Lots of umms and ahhs came
out of my mouth. I don't know what I was thinking. It was like I was
running to my Mom waiting for her to fix my problem. I was taken
aback when I was put on the spot. He sent me out to think about the
issue and come back with a recommendation. So out I went with my tail
between my legs. I don't want you to make the mistake I did, so here's
my suggestion.

You are a professional. You are being paid for your expertise, whether
you have developed any yet or not is beside the point. So, bottom line,
never bring your boss a problem without also bringing possible solutions.

1. Brainstorm the possible ways to handle your problem. The "do
    nothing" option should always be at the top of your list because it
    is the easiest resolution and more times than I would like to admit
    is the best response. The bigger the problem, the more time you
    should spend brainstorming. Being a little old fashioned, I find it
    best to brainstorm with a pencil and unlined paper. That way I
    can draw pictures and make arrows. I find using lined paper
    forces me into a more linear way of thinking. The computer has
    the same flaw. It forces you to think numerically/
    chronologically.
2. Think through the ramifications of each of your brainstormed
    ideas. Boil your thinking down to the best three possible ways to
    handle the issue.
3. Write your thinking down in a **one page** memo. The memo
    should define the problem in the first paragraph. Then present
    the top three ways to handle it. Under each of the top three
    solutions, write a one paragraph description of what you think

will happen if you pick that solution. Then in **bold** make a recommendation with your supporting arguments.

4. This memo should be on the order of four or five paragraphs. Staying brief is harder to do than you think. Writing concisely is harder than writing stream of consciousness, but this is your burden to bear not your readers. A true pro respects their client's and boss' time. It will probably take a couple revisions to boil it down to one page.

5. Unfortunately, you may get involved in a Machiavellian situation where you become the scapegoat. In that case, this memo will act as a "cover your rear" memo in the file as long as you are being reasonable. It will show, even if you're wrong, that you were thoughtful and collaborative. You were "on top" of the problem.

We are all very busy and are easily distracted. It is the nature of the world we now live in. The one page memo will easily convey the situation to your boss, client, or colleague. It will demonstrate you have thought through the problem and are doing what you are being paid to do - make recommendations. Your boss may want you to elaborate on the memo or have a discussion about it, but it is a solid starting point to efficiently come to a resolution.

Writing these memos is a great way to improve your relationship with your boss. As a boss, I hire people to help make my life easier. I bet your boss feels the same way. She doesn't want you making her life more difficult by constantly lighting fires around her. She wants you to be a firefighter with her. Writing this type of memo helps her in two ways. One, it greatly reduces the amount of time she has to think about the problem. Two, it keeps her in the loop so a good decision can be made through teamwork.

Spend the time to write a concise analysis and make a recommendation.

Uncle Mike

Mike Smith • White Owl Consulting • 612-555-5550
100 Main St, #310, Minneapolis, MN 55411 • www.WhiteOwlConsulting.com

From: msmith@whiteowlconsulting.com
Sent: Saturday, October 2, 2010 4:23 PM
To: cdoe@acme-associates.com
Subject: **Accuracy versus Precision**

Chris,
The Twins are blowing it again. I can't stand to watch anymore. I had to turn off the game. I really thought they were going to be able to win it all this year. At least the Gophers won today. I think they have finally turned around the football program.

I looked through your memo. I think you are trying to be too precise. How can you estimate down to the decimal point on that?

When you go to the bar, do they care how old you are? No. They don't care if you are 24 years, 8 months, 3 days, and 42 minutes old. They want to know if you are over 21 or under 21. It would be accurate to say you are over 21, but not precise. Detailing your real age is precise. Likewise it would still be accurate to say you are over 21, but it would be inaccurate to say you are 25 to 30 years old.

Lots of professionals get themselves into a bind with trying to be precise when they only need to be accurate. I was on a sales call with Arne, one of our technical whizzes. Arne is very smart and does great work. The client asked him if he had designed a water treatment system for a bottling plant before. Arne had done one about fifteen years ago. He went into a long story about that project and how he doesn't have any recent experience. He was very precise. We didn't win the project though.

Arne should have said yes and then asked a question or two. Maybe the client was just making small talk. Arne could have talked about a lot of similar projects that are using cutting edge technology. He probably didn't need to be precise. I am not advocating lying. I am advocating being as accurate as you need to be.

Precision is a pet peeve of mine with my industry. We often prepare forecasts of what the traffic volumes will be at an intersection during the evening rush hour in twenty years. Some consultants will say there will be 242 cars turning left between 4:45 and 5:45 p.m. on a normal Tuesday in the year 2030. I really don't know how they can do this. I say there will be 240 cars during the busiest evening hour on a normal weekday in 2030. And I think that is still a stretch. If I could predict the future that well, don't you think I'd be a billionaire by now?

Determine if you need to be precise or accurate.

Uncle Mike

Mike Smith ● White Owl Consulting ● 612-555-5550
100 Main St, #310, Minneapolis, MN 55411 ● www.WhiteOwlConsulting.com

From: msmith@whiteowlconsulting.com
Sent: Monday, October 18, 2010 4:51 PM
To: cdoe@acme-associates.com
Subject: **Don't pick your teeth**

Chris,

Congrats on joining a professional society! I hope it will be as rewarding for you is it has been for me. Remember to get involved at the committee level so you can move up to being a board member. You'll get much more out of your membership if you are actively involved.

As a professional, you'll be eating with clients and co-workers in addition to the professional society luncheons you attend. I'm not expecting you to be the second coming of Miss Manners, but there are some basics you should follow so you don't embarrass yourself. Table manners are actually supposed to make you more comfortable by providing a common playing field. Hopefully you know all of these, but there may be one or two things on the list you haven't thought about. I didn't make them up, but we all need to follow them to avoid looking like cavemen.

- Don't slurp your soup or coffee and don't make any other noises while you are eating or drinking.
- Keep your elbows off the table.
- Keep your mouth closed while you are chewing.
- If there is a bunch of silverware on the table, use the outer silverware first and use new silverware with each food course, moving to silverware closer to your plate with each course.
- Your bread plate or salad plate is at the left of your setting - at 11 o'clock if your plate was a clock. Your glass (water, wine, coffee cup) is to the right of your setting - at 1 o'clock.
- Don't pick your teeth.
- Sit up straight in your chair.
- Put your napkin in your lap when you sit down at the table.
- Excuse yourself if you need to get up from the table.
- When eating soup, move your spoon away from you in the bowl when scooping so you don't accidentally splash soup on yourself.
- Take a moment before you start eating to watch what the others are doing.
- Don't start eating until everyone at the table has been served their meal. If your meal is being held up it is polite to tell everyone

else to start. Likewise, it is ok to start if you are given "permission."

- It is common at luncheons to have items such as salad dressing, bread, butter, coffee, etc. on the table. Take an item (or not) and pass the dish/basket/bowl to your left. If someone already started everything going to the right, go with the flow. Don't cross things up.
- Always pass the salt and pepper together, even if only the salt is requested.
- Taste the food before adding salt or pepper. It is an old fashioned rule, but it says something slightly negative about you if you start dumping salt on your food before you've tasted it.
- Don't reach for items on the table; ask for them to be passed.
- If a piece of your silverware falls on the floor, try to pick it up. Whether or not you can pick it up, ask your server for a new utensil. Don't use the dropped utensil!

Bon appétit!

Uncle Mike

p.s. You are going to luncheons to meet new people. Don't sit at a table with any co-workers at it.

Mike Smith • White Owl Consulting • 612-555-5550
100 Main St, #310, Minneapolis, MN 55411 • www.WhiteOwlConsulting.com

From: msmith@whiteowlconsulting.com
Sent: Tuesday, October 19, 2010 8:51 PM
To: cdoe@acme-associates.com
Subject: **Re: Don't pick your teeth**

Chris,

That grosses me out too. If you get a piece of gristle or something else in your mouth that is bad, don't spit it into your napkin. Take it out of your mouth with the same utensil you used to get it in, set it on the edge of your plate, and if possible cover it up with a little bit of your other food.

Here are some more situational things you might run across. These pieces of etiquette are a little more obscure.

- Sara is allergic to seafood and we were at a dinner that served surf and turf. She politely inquired and all of the plates had seafood on them, which would have possibly set off a reaction for her. The kitchen graciously whipped up a chicken and pasta dish for her in about ten minutes. We would have asked in advance if we had known the menu. If you have allergy restrictions or dietary restrictions (i.e. vegetarian), try to make advanced plans. Don't throw a big fuss at the event, but you can politely ask for something else.
- At formal dinners, men stand behind their chairs until all of the ladies are seated and they also stand up when a woman leaves the table. Luncheons and most business meals are not this formal.
- When you meet a new person, it is proper to stand up to shake their hand. Two reasons why you should stand instead of staying seated - (1) you might knock something over on the table if you stay seated and (2) it presents an awkward, unbalanced situation if you stay seated and the other person is standing.
- Men - no hats at the table. Take off the sombrero.
- Do not complain about the food or the service. Ever.
- When you are finished eating, place all of your used utensils on your plate (on the right side) point down. This is a universal signal for your server to clear the plate.
- Put butter on your bread plate and put small pieces of the butter on pieces of bread/bun you have broken off. Don't butter the whole thing at once.
- At the end of the meal, say something polite - "It was nice to meet you. I hope we can do this again."

- Don't ask for a doggy bag.
- Try to order food that can be eaten with a fork. It is less messy than finger food/sandwiches.
- Make small talk, but avoid any controversial topics. At luncheons it is always great to discuss the speaker or speaking topic.
- If there is a host or hostess for the event, thank them on your way out.
- If someone is left handed in your party, seat them at the head of the table or on a left corner to increase everyone's elbow room.
- If you are eating outside of the United States, research the local customs.
- The senior person at the table picks up the tab if you are with co-workers.
- Never fight over the check. Say thank you and offer to pick up the tab next time. If you grab the check before your client, but they seem to be fighting for it – say they can pick up the tab the next time.

Practicing good etiquette should help put you at ease, not make you more nervous.

Uncle Mike

Mike Smith ● White Owl Consulting ● 612-555-5550
100 Main St, #310, Minneapolis, MN 55411 ● www.WhiteOwlConsulting.com

From: msmith@whiteowlconsulting.com
Sent: Tuesday, November 2, 2010 10:15 AM
To: cdoe@acme-associates.com
Subject: **Jargon**

Chris,
I forgot to ask – how was your Halloween party?

The LOS is forecast to degrade to F at the EB and WB TH 62/CSAH 60 interchange ramps with the proposed office building. To mitigate this poor operation, it is recommended the folded diamond be replaced with a SPUI.

Speaking in jargon makes you sound intelligent, doesn't it? Don't you think I'm a genius for writing that paragraph? Actually, I'm just poking fun at you a little bit. I didn't really understand what you are getting at in your last email. Remember, I'm not in your industry. You'll need to translate the situation into English for me before I can give you an opinion.

Professionals love jargon, especially engineers. Acronyms abound. We even label our businesses with acronyms URS, SRF, WSB, HNTB, etc. (imagine if Korunsky, Klap, and Knight started a firm?). Maybe we should all just change our company names to "Three Dead Guys." At least people will assume we have been in business for a long time if all of the founders are dead!

My friend Stuart overheard a conversation between myself and another traffic engineer. We reverted to geek speak and started using our industry's jargon. Stuart later told me it was like watching the Godfather movie when the godfather excused himself to speak Italian with one of his men. Stuart couldn't understand anything we were saying, even though he is a computer guy with an undergraduate degree in electrical engineering and a master's degree in computer science.

When you're talking to another person in your profession and you're alone, it's OK to digress into jargon. As a member of your profession, you need to know the shorthand. It's part of being a member of the club. But, you should avoid using the jargon in your memos/reports, in your presentations, or in meetings where there are people outside of your profession present (which means just about every meeting with a client). Think of your great-grandmother as your audience. She is a smart, well read lady but never went to college. She understands English, but not Italian or jargon. You should write and speak in English that Great-Grandma Betty can understand and that would pass her red-pen grandma test.

On the flip side, if someone is talking in jargon (even if it is the language of jargon you understand) in a meeting you are attending you should work to clarify what they mean. If you don't understand, ask for the layman's version.

You should jump in if you see your client's eyes glazing over because too much jargon is being used (this may happen when one of your co-workers is describing something). Restate... "you just said xxxx and that means yyyyy." Simplifying and confirming are key strategies to making sure everyone in the room is on the same page.

This takes real effort, but I promise you it will pay off later. The professionals who can explain their ideas to lay people are the most sought after.

Dump the jargon. Please translate your last email for me.

Uncle Mike

Mike Smith ● White Owl Consulting ● 612-555-5550
100 Main St, #310, Minneapolis, MN 55411 ● www.WhiteOwlConsulting.com

From: msmith@whiteowlconsulting.com
Sent: Saturday, November 20, 2010 11:03 AM
To: cdoe@acme-associates.com
Subject: **People File**

Chris,
What is the absolute best day for a salesman to call on a client?

What is the best day for you to call to say hi to a contact?

Their birthday!!!

Everyone is in a good mood on their birthday. I had a boss who took a vacation day on his birthday every year to celebrate. My mom may disagree with me - something about turning sixty. Anyway, how are you going to call, send an email, or a card if you don't know when their birthday is?

I recommend you keep a people file. There are different software packages to help you track your contacts (when you last talked with them, important data on them, etc.). You could also build a simple spreadsheet. Or it can be as simple as a few notes on the back of their business card in your rolodex. The key is to develop a system that you will use.

Things to put in your database:
- All of the contact information from the person's business card.
- Their birthday.
- Kids and spouse information.
- General interests outside of work.
- Role in their current job.
- Past employers.
- Alma mater.
- Favorite sports teams.
- Hobbies.
- Interesting travels.
- Tracking of each time you contact them.
- The last project you worked on with them.

LinkedIn and Facebook are good places to get information. Don't be overt in discussions with your contacts. You don't want to appear to be filling out a questionnaire. Or worse – seem like a stalker. But you should keep track of details as they come up. It's part of being a thoughtful person.

There are two ways to use your contact database. One is to keep track of reasons to get in touch with people, i.e. to say Happy Birthday. The other is to look through it when you are going to a meeting or a luncheon. Go through the people you think you will bump into.

You will look very thoughtful if you can remember details of past conversations. It's very flattering if you can say something like, "Joanne - last time I saw you, I think you mentioned your daughter was starting first grade. How is she doing?" These are the types of questions we would be able to pull off the cuff if we had perfect memories. I don't have a perfect memory, so my people file helps me remember the personal things.

Keep your contact database current and use it.

Uncle Mike

Mike Smith • White Owl Consulting • 612-555-5550
100 Main St, #310, Minneapolis, MN 55411 • www.WhiteOwlConsulting.com

From: msmith@whiteowlconsulting.com
Sent: Tuesday, December 7, 2010 4:01 PM
To: cdoe@acme-associates.com
Subject: **Jake the Ball Hog**

Chris,
Where is your company party going to be this year? I know they have an open bar, but stay sober.

You finally met "Jake the Ball Hog." Most offices have one. A guy who doesn't collaborate well. A guy who protects his turf at all costs. Jake the Ball Hog is usually very insecure. He thinks building walls will make him more valuable. The company will never get rid of him if there are things that only he can do.

Jake the Ball Hog doesn't realize everyone is replaceable. We force ourselves to replace the president of our country every eight years and sometimes we fire him after four years. The CEO's of Fortune 500 companies are replaceable. You and I are replaceable. Jake is definitely replaceable.

Unfortunately, your boss puts up with Jake being a kingdom builder. This isn't good for your team and it isn't good for you. You need to be exposed to all facets of your profession. You need to work to break down the walls Jake has put up. There are two approaches you can take.

One – you can try to convince your boss to help you go around Jake. This is usually unsuccessful. Your boss doesn't want to deal with Jake, or she wouldn't let him be a Ball Hog in the first place.

Two – the preferable option – is to slowly convince Jake that he should open up to you. You aren't going to knock his protective wall down by using a battering ram. You need to be the slow drip that wears a crack in the wall. This takes a lot of patience. You need to be very methodical. You need to be your nice, approachable self. Jake needs to get comfortable with you. You need to neutralize any threat he may feel from you. This can take months.

Over time you'll start to see little opportunities where you can be helpful. You need to offer to help whenever you see one of these opportunities.

He may say no to you the first twenty times you offer, but there will be a time he is in a huge bind and he'll decide to take a chance on you. Once you are in, you need to deliver. After you have your opening, you need to be as thoughtful and honest as you can be. Your ultimate goal is to become a trusted assistant. The one person Jake the Ball Hog goes to for advice.

On a personal level, I hope you are never a Ball Hog. If you are seen as irreplaceable, you'll never get promoted because your boss won't want to try to fill your shoes.

When you come across someone protecting their turf, you need to be patient and kill them with kindness.

Uncle Mike

Mike Smith • White Owl Consulting • 612-555-5550
100 Main St, #310, Minneapolis, MN 55411 • www.WhiteOwlConsulting.com

From: msmith@whiteowlconsulting.com
Sent: Tuesday, December 21, 2010 7:22 AM
To: cdoe@acme-associates.com
Subject: **Answering Questions**

Chris,
Don't panic! You can't help it that your boss is out with appendicitis.
Focus on getting through the meeting as her stand-in. It's an internal
meeting, so there isn't a lot of pressure on you. Luckily your boss has
had you take the lead in a few internal meetings with her in attendance.
You'll do fine. It will be a little different though because you are now the
"lead" expert and don't have your boss to lean on. You'll probably have
to answer a few questions you would normally let her handle.

I was in a public hearing for a residential subdivision project. After my
presentation on the traffic issues and our plan, a member of the audience
paraded up a group of kids and asked the city council members which of
the kids should be killed by all of the traffic that will be put on their
street. This guy went into an impassioned speech wondering how many
kids would need to be killed before we'd do something about it. I calmly
stood up and explained that one dead kid would be a random event, two
dead kids would be a coincidence, but three dead kids would be a
statistically significant pattern that we would have to address. OK, I
didn't say this, but it crossed my mind.

I hear the dead kid argument more than I would like. It is a powerfully
emotional argument, but I dug through the crash statistic database for the
whole state and it turns out pedestrian crashes are very rare. As an
engineer, there are no statistically significant ways to argue a cause/effect
situation when it comes to these types of crashes. I am prepared with
data as well as a couple of stories when this topic comes up.

As a professional you will often be put on the spot. You are the expert in
the room, so people are going to ask you questions about your area of
expertise. Sometimes the questions will be nicely asked because the
person is genuinely interested in what you have to say. Other times the
questions will be more hostile - asked only to advance an agenda. Those
situations will make you feel like you are a witness being examined on
the stand.

Being prepared really sunk in after my second cousin Marge's wedding. It was shortly after 9/11. I think it was the Saturday right after. Marge's brother Eddie is a police officer. He stood up and said a prayer for the emergency responders in New York. Then he asked my grandpa to come up and lead us in singing God Bless America (Grandpa is a great singer and did the singing in the wedding ceremony). Grandpa popped up and sang it perfectly. Later I told him how impressed I was. I don't think I could get all of the words right, let alone hit the notes if I was put on the spot. He said he thought he might be asked to sing something patriotic, so he practiced the Star Spangled Banner and God Bless America several times that morning just in case. A true professional.

The key to surviving, and hopefully thriving, in these situations is to be prepared. You should be able to speak off the cuff on the basics of your profession. If you are an accountant, you should be able to explain credits and debits on the spot. If you are a mechanical engineer, you should be able to explain torque.

Prepare answers for all of the questions you think you could be asked.

Uncle Mike

Mike Smith ● White Owl Consulting ● 612-555-5550
100 Main St, #310, Minneapolis, MN 55411 ● www.WhiteOwlConsulting.com

From: msmith@whiteowlconsulting.com
Sent: Wednesday, December 22, 2010 9:08 PM
To: cdoe@acme-associates.com
Subject: **Re: Answering Questions**

Chris,
It's almost Christmas, so everyone will be in a good mood at the meeting. No worries.

That story has a great kernel of truth in it, but you should expand it. Remember, the best answers are a lot like Aesop's fables. They give a related story and then draw a conclusion based on the story. If you can tell a sixty second story followed with an "and that makes me think...." fifteen second answer, you will be remembered a lot more than if you jump right to the punch line. Stories pull us in. Talking about a similar experience and what you learned is much better than just saying what you learned. Talking about similar situations will also establish your credibility as the expert.

Make sure you memorize as many of your facts as you can. For better or worse we equate good memories with being smart. You will look like a professional if you can answer questions without having to look through your files.

This is not a license to make things up. You may be tempted to stretch what you know and make a guess. These little white lies can really bite you later on. If you truly don't know the answer you should say so. Say you want to be sure to get them the right answer and you'll get back to them tomorrow (or later if you can't deliver tomorrow). Also, bring your files with so you are prepared to look up information on the spot. Prepare as much as you can for the meeting, but don't be afraid to say you don't know something.

It's better to get back to someone with an answer than be caught in a lie.

Uncle Mike

Mike Smith ● White Owl Consulting ● 612-555-5550
100 Main St, #310, Minneapolis, MN 55411 ● www.WhiteOwlConsulting.com

From: msmith@whiteowlconsulting.com
Sent: Monday, January 3, 2011 8:48 PM
To: cdoe@acme-associates.com
Subject: **The World Wide Web**

Chris,

I saw that you added pictures from your weekend to your Facebook page. You're making me jealous (and feel old). Your New Year's Eve party looked a lot more exciting than mine. It looks like you updated your Facebook from work today.

When I was in high school I was addicted to my Nintendo – yes, I'm that old. I spent hours in front of the TV playing games. When I went to college, games like Doom were very popular. Then, right after I graduated, all of my buddies were playing Warcraft.

I don't know about you, but video games are like kryptonite for me. They make me weak. I could easily waste a lot of hours. So, in college, I avoided computer games like the plague. I was afraid I would get too sucked in. In spite of my best efforts, I still managed to have too much fun a few quarters.

Your aunt is addicted to Facebook at the moment. She is like someone who can't stop playing the slots. She keeps going over to her laptop expecting really exciting things to be posted – like the slot machine player who can't stop pulling the handle because they are one pull away from the big payout.

I don't have any problems with Facebook or most of the things happening in cyberspace as long as you control them. If I had been born thirty years earlier, I would have needed a large library of reference books and about five technicians working with me to produce the same volume of work I crank out today. This leap in productivity is due to computers and the internet. They are amazingly useful tools.

But I want you to keep in mind that surfing the internet at work is a very bad habit. It can suck hours of your productivity. On top of it, some companies monitor their employee's web usage. Too much time on Facebook is a really dumb reason to get fired. And never look at porn at work. I know two people in my sphere of contacts that were caught by their employers and lost their jobs. If you are a work time surfer, you have to figure out how to break the habit. If you don't surf at work, don't start.

Don't surf at work.

Uncle Mike

p.s. I assume you know this, but make sure all of your online info is protected by invite only viewing. Your co-workers don't need to see those party photos of you (your mom probably doesn't need to see all of them either).

Mike Smith ● White Owl Consulting ● 612-555-5550
100 Main St, #310, Minneapolis, MN 55411 ● www.WhiteOwlConsulting.com

From: msmith@whiteowlconsulting.com
Sent: Saturday, January 8, 2011 9:32 AM
To: cdoe@acme-associates.com
Subject: **<u>Your Product</u>**

Chris,

I flipped through your report. I don't have much to add technically since I am not in your field, but your analysis and conclusions seem to make sense. I'm a little surprised by the format and lack of color/graphics. Remember, a picture is worth a thousand words.

It's pretty easy to look at a plumber's work. When the doors open on the back of a semi, you can see what the trucker is delivering. What do professionals produce? Thoughts. We document those thoughts on paper and increasingly in electronic files that are never printed. So what do the documents you produce look like? Does that 30 page report look like it is worth $20,000? Add pictures, tables, graphs, color and well written text to bring your story to life.

Your client assumes you are doing good work - that you are producing good thoughts. You need to convey those thoughts. Some consultants in my industry produce reports that visually look worse than the reports being produced in my kids' elementary school. Software packages make it so easy to put together a great looking report, spreadsheet, drawing, etc. Why wouldn't we use color pictures to illustrate our points? Why follow the report outline your firm developed fifty years ago on a typewriter?

A few basics about reports, which are amazingly neglected:
1. Proofread your document. Make sure the grammar and spelling are correct.
2. You should be so blessed to have someone in your office like my co-worker Mary. Have her read your document. She'll do a better job proofreading than you do. Plus she'll challenge you if something doesn't make sense. Find your Mary in the office and become close friends.
3. If you have any kind of math involved in your document, make sure it is right.
4. Step back and actually question your analysis. Is it correct? Any holes in your logic?

5. If you have tables and/or figures, use a progressive numbering convention and label them consistently. You'll look like an amateur if your figure numbering is off or if you decide to use different fonts and point sizes on different tables.
6. If you are incorporating other people's work into your document, scrutinize it. It is too easy to assume they adequately checked through their work.
7. Write to your audience. If you aren't sure who might be looking at your document, make sure a sixth grader can understand it.
8. Make clear recommendations. As a professional, you have a duty. Don't shirk your responsibility with "on this hand/then on this hand" type debate that tries to cover your rear end without making a recommendation. You should fully document the situation, but give your reader your interpretation.
9. Learn how to use your software packages. If you are making a pdf with Adobe's Acrobat, put in bookmarks and make the document easy to navigate.
10. If you are going to have your report printed, don't use the cheesy big plastic comb bindings. Spend a little more money to produce a classy looking report.

Make your reports look like a million bucks.

Uncle Mike

Mike Smith ● White Owl Consulting ● 612-555-5550
100 Main St, #310, Minneapolis, MN 55411 ● www.WhiteOwlConsulting.com

From: msmith@whiteowlconsulting.com
Sent: Friday, January 28, 2011 4:39 PM
To: cdoe@acme-associates.com
Subject: **Tempers**

Chris,
I have had a few co-workers blow up in meetings. One guy I worked with, Vern the Volcano, was a notorious hot head. Blowing up can be an effective communications strategy if it is well thought out in advance. Unfortunately most people boil over because they lost their cool without any advance thought. I don't think Vern the Volcano was very premeditated. Not a good situation.

Cut your Vern the Volcano some slack. The holidays can be tough on people. Maybe he has a bad family situation. It is a good rule of thumb to always assume there is some underlying reason behind people's bad behavior.

For the first couple of years of the Civil War the Union was losing. They were losing in embarrassing ways. A lot of it had to do with inept leadership in the army. Several of Abraham Lincoln's letters to his generals surfaced after his death. These were very emotional letters lambasting the generals and their poor decisions. As you can imagine, Lincoln was really mad when a general with overwhelming numbers of troops and firepower would let the Confederates retreat instead of cutting them off.

The really interesting thing about these letters is that they were found in Lincoln's personal belongings after his assassination. He never sent them. It turns out Lincoln made a practice of expressing his emotions in letters to vent his frustrations. Then he wouldn't send them.

Abe was a very eloquent man. His speeches were the reason he was elected. As a young man he used his wit and oratory skills to rip down his opponents. His thinking evolved and he stopped this practice.

Lincoln is arguably America's greatest president. Not only did he win a war, he laid the groundwork for reconciling the union. He did this by leading. Nothing very constructive would have come from his nasty letters except making him feel better in the moment. He knew that. We should learn from him.

Lincoln's habit of writing letters of anger and then not sending them (or better yet, destroying them) is a practice all of us should use. It dissipates the pressure of anger while preserving your relationships. A caution - these things are best handwritten. Emails can be sent by accident. Files on your computer can be found. Shredded or burnt paper goes away.

You can never take back something you say in a moment of anger. Even if you apologize and they accept your apology, what you said will still be in the back of the person's head. Assume people will remember and resent your angry words for the rest of their lives.

Keep your cool.

Uncle Mike

Mike Smith • White Owl Consulting • 612-555-5550
100 Main St, #310, Minneapolis, MN 55411 • www.WhiteOwlConsulting.com

From: msmith@whiteowlconsulting.com
Sent: Thursday, February 17, 2011 5:39 PM
To: cdoe@acme-associates.com
Subject: **YES to new opportunities!**

Chris,
That sounds like a great opportunity. It will expand the types of things you are working on. You should definitely jump at the chance.

A few months into my career one of the company vice-presidents came to me and asked if I would handle the annual paperwork required so our client cities could get their little slice of the gas tax. I'm sure my boss was involved with the decision and I don't remember how much free will I had to say no, but my immediate response was a very enthusiastic Yes! I would come to learn this paperwork really was a pain in the neck and there was a lot of red tape to be negotiated. There was a pretty significant learning curve. Do I regret saying yes? No way!

I was taking over for a guy who had been doing this paperwork for about a decade and no one else in the firm was up to speed on this minutia. I was only months into my career, but I was working with the head honchos at our client cities because getting this money was very important to them. I was working with the firm's top twelve biggest clients. They usually don't talk to first year engineers.

I think some other young engineers over the years passed on this or they started and then quit. This was a mistake for them because they could have raised their profile in the firm. I did. City engineers would call me asking about their gas tax money directly. They didn't go through the senior management. This was great for the firm and it was great for me. I was seen as a helpful resource for our biggest clients.

Fast forward about three years and I was applying to become the traffic engineer for a suburb named Riverside. This was a very good position but I didn't have all the qualifications they wanted. One of the responsibilities of the newly created position was to do the gas tax paperwork for the city. Having a lot of experience with this paperwork gave me a leg up on my competition and it helped me land the job.

In turn, working for Riverside gave me a lot of credibility when I was later marketing my own start-up firm. This stepping stone in my career was partly due to me saying yes to learning the gas tax paperwork.

There are a lot of books written about positive attitudes and how beneficial it is to stay positive. It isn't all happy talk. Attitude really does matter. I think (and hope) you are a positive person. Whether you are or not, your co-workers and clients should think you are a positive person - especially your boss. Early in my career I developed the habit of asking "how can I help?" I would ask this question when my boss called me into his office. I also would proactively ask when I could tell my boss was stressed out. Now that I'm the boss, I don't get to ask this question very much inside the firm. But I still try to use the phrase "what can I do to help you" when my clients call.

If you use these helpful phrases and deliver what you promise, your co-workers and clients are going to start to lean on you. And as you become a reliable resource, you will accelerate the opportunities available to you.

Make it a habit of asking "how can I help?"

Uncle Mike

Mike Smith • White Owl Consulting • 612-555-5550
100 Main St, #310, Minneapolis, MN 55411 • www.WhiteOwlConsulting.com

From: msmith@whiteowlconsulting.com
Sent: Friday, February 18, 2011 7:54 AM
To: cdoe@acme-associates.com
Subject: **<u>Saying NO!</u>**

Chris,
I should have given you a caveat in that last email! In the specific case we were talking about you should say yes. But eventually you'll sometimes need to say no.

I just tried to convince you to be helpful and open to new opportunities. How am I going to resolve saying yes and saying no? Good question. Like a typical consultant, I'm going to start out by saying "it depends." For the first few years of your career I want you to take advantage of as many opportunities as you can. Unexpected situations are going to present themselves, even if they look more like problems than opportunities at the time. Saying yes to new opportunities will help speed up your on the job education and this is education you are getting paid for.

Here is a practical point though - most brutally evident in law firms where you are expected to make partner in three to five years. In a lot of law firms, you aren't going to make partner unless you bring in a certain "book of business." You have to create enough business to keep you going plus cover your overhead at a minimum. You might be expected to keep some of the associates busy too. To move to a senior partnership role you will certainly need to keep associates billable on your cases. This sets up a tension with always saying yes.

A senior partner may come in and ask you to sit on a committee or do some type of non-billable administrative project. A bunch of the partners may love your work and be very happy with you. If the only criteria for becoming a partner is developing your own book of business though, this administrative stuff is hurting you instead of helping you. The partners are probably passing it to you so they can focus on their marketing efforts.

Once you are on the bubble of partnership when it comes to the amount of time you have been with the firm, saying yes to these administrative projects may also have an insidious side effect. The partners are not treating you like an equal - like a partner. They are treating you as a junior. Once you are competent as a professional, you need to work very hard to project your professionalism. Saying no may actually make you look more like a partner.

You need to decide if saying yes or no is right. Early on in your career, say yes immediately while you are building your image. You want to be a go-to guy. A few years into your career, after you have established your image, you'll want to start transitioning to a person who is helpful yet busy (caveat - when dealing with clients or your direct boss always try to help as fast as you can). Say something like - "I really want to help and that sounds like a very exciting project. Can I get back to you tomorrow? I have a lot on my plate and need to make sure I can commit 100% percent to the project." Then truly think about the project. Consider carefully if it's something that could be good for your career.

Never rudely dismiss someone's request for help. Burning bridges is almost always a bad idea as a professional. You are working in a pretty small community and word will get around.

Know when to say no and say it tactfully.

Uncle Mike

Mike Smith ● White Owl Consulting ● 612-555-5550
100 Main St, #310, Minneapolis, MN 55411 ● www.WhiteOwlConsulting.com

From: msmith@whiteowlconsulting.com
Sent: Friday, March 11, 2011 4:18 PM
To: cdoe@acme-associates.com
Subject: **Mistakes**

Chris,

Take a deep breath. Don't let this ruin your weekend (and the St. Patrick's Day party you are going to). We all make mistakes.

I was doing a traffic study for one of my repeat clients. I was working in a city where I had already done several traffic studies. We were in a hurry so I pulled together the study as fast as I could. It turns out the city had a performance standard higher than the industry norm for a specific situation I hadn't run across before. I missed it and my study didn't conform to this standard. I was sloppy.

It turned out to be a big deal when the developer submitted my study to the city. This was a big mistake on my part. It shouldn't have happened and it made my client look bad. I first apologized profusely and then worked through the night to revise my study to conform to the correct standard. My client appreciated (1) that I apologized and (2) that I immediately worked to fix the mistake. We were able to get past the mistake and the development turned out fine. Since then I have worked for them on several more projects.

I had an intern work for me a few years ago. He made a number crunching mistake a couple of months after he started. Not a huge issue because our quality control process (double checking) caught the mistake. He said sorry. The next month he made a similar mistake. He shrugged his shoulders and again said he was sorry. Clearly the mistake still wasn't a big deal to him. It would have been a big deal to me if it slipped through our double checking and our client caught the mistake.

I accept that everyone makes mistakes and I'm pretty easy going, but I was upset that he blew it off. Any chance he had of working for me in the future was gone. Not because he made a mistake but because he didn't learn from that mistake (and he didn't seem to care).

You will continue to make mistakes on the job. We all make mistakes. I still do. That is why we have systems in place to catch them. The difference is in how you react when you do make a mistake. Here is what you should do:

1. Apologize to your boss. If you have direct contact with a client, apologize to them too. Really be sorry (but don't sound defeated). Your body language and voice will communicate a lot more than your words.

2. Work as hard as you can to fix the problem. You may need to come up with several alternatives for fixing the problem. Do the best you possibly can. Explain the ramifications of your mistake. Go back to that email I sent you on one page memos for guidance.

3. Learn your lesson. Don't make the same mistake again. You'll blow your credibility and relationship if you do.

It's not being perfect that matters, it's taking responsibility for and then learning from your mistake that helps you grow.

Uncle Mike

Mike Smith ● White Owl Consulting ● 612-555-5550
100 Main St, #310, Minneapolis, MN 55411 ● www.WhiteOwlConsulting.com

From: msmith@whiteowlconsulting.com
Sent: Sunday, April 3, 2011 4:23 PM
To: cdoe@acme-associates.com
Subject: **Office Politics & Romances**

Chris,
Slow down tiger! Your brother told me you are starting to date someone you work with. Danger! Danger!

Two of my acquaintances at Bloomfield were married. My memory about the situation is a little shaky. I don't remember if they were married when they started their career or if they met on the job. The partners at the firm were pretty old school, so I don't think they would have hired a man and a woman out of college who were married. I'm guessing they met at work and then got married. About a year after they were married, they got divorced. Ouch. The woman quit and went to work at another firm. This was obviously an extreme case, but no matter how things shake out I don't think office romances work very well.

If your dating starts to take a serious turn, one of you should plan to quit in short order. I don't think your company is big enough to get a lateral transfer far enough away from her. OK, I'll get off of my soapbox now. There is a chance you could make it work. But go into this thoughtfully.

Here is my quick corollary on office politics. In an anti-Nike way, I am going to say - Just Don't Do It. Your goal at this stage in your career should be to become competent in your profession and not be seen as distracted by anything or anyone. It's a big world and there are a lot of great women out there who don't work at Acme.

Weigh the risks of your office romance and don't let your heart bias the scale.

Uncle Mike

p.s. To be safe, look up Acme's policies on office relationships and sexual harassment. Hopefully it's still ok to pay a nice compliment.

Mike Smith ● White Owl Consulting ● 612-555-5550
100 Main St, #310, Minneapolis, MN 55411 ● www.WhiteOwlConsulting.com

From: msmith@whiteowlconsulting.com
Sent: Thursday, April 21, 2011 9:03 PM
To: cdoe@acme-associates.com
Subject: **The Storyteller**

Chris,
I guess it's officially spring. A bunch of golf courses opened up last weekend. I am sneaking out at lunch tomorrow to hit the driving range. Can you make time to join me?

Interesting observation. I think you're right, usually upper management types are "good talkers." I met two Tonys early in my career. Both good guys in their early 30s. Both engineers. But they were on very different career paths. Tony One was jovial in the office but didn't like dealing with clients or working out of the office. He became an engineer because he liked designing things and that was what he was going to do. He sat behind his computer 8 to 10 hours a day. He was competent, but he wasn't a genius.

Tony Two was also a competent engineer. He wasn't a genius either. Tony Two liked people a little more than Tony One and became a key contact for a few of the firm's smaller clients. He was a geeky engineer like me and needed to work on his communication skills. So he joined Toastmasters and worked on giving speeches.

Tony One ruffled some of management's feathers and it was a pretty easy decision to let him go when the economy soured. Competent designers are replaceable. Tony Two is still with the firm and his clients have grown. His stature in the firm has grown too. He is on solid footing since rainmakers are usually the last folks to be let go. Even if it is somewhat against your nature, I hope you see the wisdom in being like Tony Two. You'll enjoy your career a lot more and you'll have more opportunities.

Think about the people at the top of your profession and you'll notice almost all of them have one trait in common. They pass the grandma test - they can sit down with your 92 year old great-grandmother and explain their expertise to her in a way she understands. They drop the jargon and speak in plain English. They usually use stories and analogies to make their point.

I want you to become a passable storyteller so you can communicate with anyone. The easiest first step you can take is to join Toastmasters and progress in their program. Toastmaster clubs provide a safe environment that will teach you how to speak in a time tested manner. I was a member for five years and gave over twenty speeches. The program destroyed my phobia (which was big) of talking in front of people.

The second step you can take is to start to talk like a storyteller when you are trying to make a point. Here is an easy formula to follow that was perfected by Aesop and is used by every comic book:
1. The story is about a hero.
2. The hero faces some adversity, which they may or may not overcome.
3. There is a one or two sentence lesson to be learned from the hero's actions.

A simple example - instead of an accountant telling a client they need to pay their payroll taxes on time, they tell this story. "One of my clients, Rob, faced a similar situation and he decided not to pay the payroll taxes. He wanted to hold the cash for an upcoming opportunity. Rob forgot to pay the payroll taxes even though his big opportunity didn't materialize. He was audited and he ended up paying pretty big fines. I hope you can find a way to get these paid on time." OK, it's a cheesy example, but try to soften things and put your advice into perspective by using analogies.

Go tell a story!

Uncle Mike

Mike Smith ● White Owl Consulting ● 612-555-5550
100 Main St, #310, Minneapolis, MN 55411 ● www.WhiteOwlConsulting.com

From: msmith@whiteowlconsulting.com
Sent: Saturday, May 7, 2011 10:41 AM
To: Chris@gmail.com
Subject: **You're Out of a Job**

Chris,
The economy is hitting a rough patch. Do yourself a favor and do a little contingency planning this weekend. Also – don't forget to get your mom flowers tomorrow for Mother's Day.

There are three different reasons people are forced out of work. One - your employer's overall business plan doesn't support you, i.e. the economy is in the tank and they don't need or can't afford your position. Usually this is called being laid off, not fired. Two - you aren't right for the position and your performance reflects it. This is usually called being fired. Three – you do something blatantly against company policy. This is definitely called being fired. Being without a job is something most people don't think about in advance, but hopefully these few paragraphs will stick in your mind just in case it ever happens to you.

You should see layoffs coming. The economy is bad. The partner you work for just left and there isn't someone to feed you work. The company just lost its best client. Your biggest competitor is off-shoring your type of work to India – will your company follow suit? If you see any of these things, start thinking about your exit strategy. Keep your resume up to date and talk to people in your network. Listen to those pesky recruiters if they call. They can be helpful. Regularly look at job postings.

I think I talked to you about keeping a copy of your contact database at home, but this is especially important if you feel layoffs coming. Backup your Outlook file once a week so you have your contacts and email. If you are laid off you may be escorted straight to the door without a chance to go back to your cube. Think about what other information would be valuable to have if you just got booted to the street. Client lists, past proposals, cost estimating spreadsheets, procedures, checklists, past reports/memos, etc. I'm not a lawyer and I'm certainly not advocating doing anything illegal or unethical. Just think it through.

If you are laid off or fired, switch to negotiation mode. Your boss is going to be feeling some level of guilt. Ask for a severance package. Ask for more money. Ask for a reference letter. Ask to keep your laptop. Ask for job placement services. Ask to work part time in the office for a few more weeks (it might be easier to land another job quickly if you can honestly say you are still employed at Acme).

As hard as it will be, shut off the emotions and try to think like a sports agent (or a toddler). You have some emotional leverage. Negotiate with your boss or whoever is laying you off. You can also go higher up the chain of command to negotiate. You can also try to negotiate with HR too. You'll probably get more out of people who know you and like you (hopefully your boss). Do it right away while everyone is nervous and has a lot of anxiety. Don't wait until their emotions die down.

And remember, if you ever do get laid off, you are early in your career. You have plenty of time to bounce back. A lot of people have been laid off and it was only a small bump in their career path. Take a deep breath and treat finding a job like a job. Put in the hard work and prove you are a professional.

As the boy scouts say – be prepared.

Uncle Mike

Mike Smith ● White Owl Consulting ● 612-555-5550
100 Main St, #310, Minneapolis, MN 55411 ● www.WhiteOwlConsulting.com

From: msmith@whiteowlconsulting.com
Sent: Sunday, May 8, 2011 8:36 PM
To: Chris@gmail.com
Subject: **Re: You're Out of a Job**

Chris,

OK, OK – things are going fine at Acme. You don't see layoffs coming. Make sure you think this through and it isn't a quick reaction. One more thought...

Hopefully, you'll never be fired because of your performance. You shouldn't be. The company and your boss have a vested interest in making sure you are successful. You seem to be off to a great start. Your boss should be reviewing your performance periodically and working with you to develop your talents. If she is less than 100% happy, you should be working together to improve your performance.

Whether or not you are having these discussions, I want you to spend some time thinking about your job. Critically assess your situation. The position might not have turned out to be a good fit for you. It happens. You owe it to yourself and your employer to do good work and you should work somewhere you can do your best.

If you think it's time to plan for a change (either because the job fit wasn't the best or other factors seem to suggest you may be laid off) - start looking! It's much easier to get a job when you have a job. You'll feel less pressure, which will help you perform better in the interviewing process.

Also, there will be less competition if you switch jobs before a lot of people in your position get laid off. Just make sure you aren't leaving the Titanic for a leaking life raft. Do your best to only go to work for companies that are well positioned. My father-in-law had a co-worker who left Target to work at Best Buy because she knew layoffs were coming at Target. Her whole team at Target survived the layoff and she was caught in a layoff at Best Buy three weeks after she started. Ouch!

Make sure you aren't a square peg trying to fit into a round hole.

Uncle Mike

Mike Smith ● White Owl Consulting ● 612-555-5550
100 Main St, #310, Minneapolis, MN 55411 ● www.WhiteOwlConsulting.com

From: msmith@whiteowlconsulting.com
Sent: Tuesday, May 24, 2011 4:39 PM
To: cdoe@acme-associates.com
Subject: **In Over Your Head**

Chris,
You're sure you can't work sixteen hours a day for the next ten days and get that project done? Deep breath…. if you truly can't get it done, you need to go talk to your boss.

I assume you have done your soul searching and truly have no way of getting your project done on time. Is it because it can't be done at all or because you don't have enough time? Would help from a co-worker or a more senior person help?

Break down your project into the individual tasks that have to get done. Put a check by all of the ones you can do. If there are any you can't do, try to identify who you think could do them. Figure out what tasks could be done simultaneously if you could get someone helping you. Figure out your critical path – which tasks have to be done one after the other. Lay out a plan for doing tasks that has you working twelve hours a day, seven days a week. Make sure you are doing as many of the critical path items as possible. Then identify which tasks you won't be able to do, how long you think each one should take, who you think could do it for you, and when you need each task done.

Sketch this all out on a pad of paper and go talk to your boss. Explain how you are in over your head and you need her help. Lay out your plan and ask for her advice. It's very important to show you will be working very hard right up until the project is done. Also apologize (sincerely) for not foreseeing your problem sooner. She may be able to get you the additional resources you need or adjust the schedule. Come to an agreement on your plan and get to work.

I hope you learned a lesson through all of this. You need to make promises you know you can keep.

This isn't the end of the world. You'll get better at managing your work. And please learn how to get your work done in about forty hours a week as soon as possible. There will occasionally be a crisis that will require you to put in some long hours, but you do need some balance in your life.

Never surprise your boss.

Uncle Mike

Mike Smith • White Owl Consulting • 612-555-5550
100 Main St, #310, Minneapolis, MN 55411 • www.WhiteOwlConsulting.com

From: msmith@whiteowlconsulting.com
Sent: Wednesday, June 8, 2011 1:36 PM
To: cdoe@acme-associates.com
Subject: **Your Education**

Chris,
Happy Anniversary! Does it feel like you have been with Acme for two years? I just got back from a half day seminar and am charged up. The details would bore you, but the speaker gave me a new way of looking at a situation I run into regularly. While you don't have a license that requires continuing education credits like I do, I think you should look into seminars and other education to help expand the way you look at problems.

You spent a lot of time and money (at least your parent's money) to get your degree. Congratulations on making it! But your real education is just beginning.

I've talked to architects, attorneys, accountants, and engineers and most of them agree with my assessment of a professional degree. It teaches you to think like a member of your professional community. My degree taught me to think like an engineer. It gave me a vocabulary and a methodology for tackling problems. Unfortunately, it taught me to see the proverbial trees but not the forest. As I started working on projects, I started putting together the pieces. My projects had nuggets of things I learned in several different classes, but no professor ever took a step back to put it all together. Putting these things together is the focus of your first couple of years on the job.

Continuing education, as required for a lot of professional licenses and certifications, helps you put the pieces together so you can see the forest for the trees. Seminars will also fill in gaps in your education (some practical ideas aren't rigorous enough to be covered in our ivory tower universities). I don't want you to blow this off. Hopefully your employer will support some amount of ongoing training.

First, try to get training on the software packages you use. I assume you know how to use word processing and spreadsheet programs by now. If not, you should definitely start there. Try to get into advanced classes.

The introductory classes are usually for people who didn't grow up with computers. You can probably teach the introductory class at this point.

Once you are good on the software packages you use, try to branch out to intellectual classes. Try to go to one seminar a year that lasts one to three days. The one hour luncheons you might be able to attend will be interesting and are great for networking. But you aren't going to get into a topic unless you spend some real time on it. A good example of this is the environmental movement going on right now. Architects and engineers are scrambling to take classes on making their designs "greener." Becoming LEED certified is a hot topic.

While you are looking for classes to take, I want you to join Toastmasters if you haven't already. You will have to talk in front of a group if you want to be a professional. Toastmasters is hands down the simplest way to become a competent speaker.

Lastly, your continuing education is a big topic you should talk through with your boss (since hopefully she is authorizing the time and money for you to do this). Try to craft a yearly plan for the type of training you want to get. Laying out a plan will make it more likely you'll get the funding and time out of the office approved. There will always be something going on at the last minute that will make it less than ideal for you to be off at a training seminar. Having an agreed upon yearly plan will make it harder for your boss to tell you to skip this seminar because of an emergency fire drill.

Join Toastmasters!

Uncle Mike

Mike Smith • White Owl Consulting • 612-555-5550
100 Main St, #310, Minneapolis, MN 55411 • www.WhiteOwlConsulting.com

From: msmith@whiteowlconsulting.com
Sent: Thursday, June 9, 2011 7:15 AM
To: cdoe@acme-associates.com
Subject: **Raise Time**

Chris,

I almost forgot, it's time to ask for your raise.   Write a memo
documenting what you have achieved compared with the plan you laid
out a year ago. Close the memo by asking for a raise. Ask for at least
20%, but don't go over 40%. Base it on the research you have been
doing. Bring the memo to your annual review with your boss or set up a
special meeting with her. If she balks at the raise, which she may, have a
counter offer ready. Maybe the company could pay for you to get an
MBA, send you to a national conference, or give you more flexible work
hours. Then ask what it takes to get a significant raise again in a few
years.

Remember the big caveat on this – if times are tough for the company,
don't ask for a raise. Be grateful for the job.

Ask for a significant raise at your second anniversary.

Uncle Mike

Mike Smith • White Owl Consulting • 612-555-5550
100 Main St, #310, Minneapolis, MN 55411 • www.WhiteOwlConsulting.com

From: msmith@whiteowlconsulting.com
Sent: Friday, June 17, 2011 4:53 PM
To: cdoe@acme-associates.com
Subject: **Re: Rob Quit**

Chris,
Sorry to hear that. I know you got to be friends with Rob. I am sure you'll miss grabbing lunch with him. He worked in another department, so his quitting shouldn't affect your work much. The company softball team has a hole to fill now. Be happy for him and stay in touch with him.

This is a good time to say this again – the company doesn't love you. Companies are neutral entities. They aren't good or bad (people working in them are) – companies themselves just are. I am an owner in my company and it doesn't love me either (I still forget this every once in a while though). When you need love, go to your family. This is harsh, but don't invest a lot of your wellbeing in the company. Take pride in your work - yes - but don't let it consume you.

This emotional neutrality includes not getting too close with your co-workers. Someday you'll be upper management. You'll be putting yourself in some very awkward positions if you are managing your best friend, or worse – need to lay them off. Make your lifetime friends out of people you'll never work with.

I am not saying you should be an ogre at work. You should be friendly. You should even be involved in some of the after-hours activities with your co-workers. But do not become close friends with them.

You may love your company, but remember it is incapable of loving you back.

Uncle Mike

p.s. Don't forget Father's Day is coming up.

Mike Smith ● White Owl Consulting ● 612-555-5550
100 Main St, #310, Minneapolis, MN 55411 ● www.WhiteOwlConsulting.com

From: msmith@whiteowlconsulting.com
Sent: Thursday, June 23, 2011 9:54 PM
To: cdoe@acme-associates.com
Subject: **Loyalty**

Chris,
So you got a loyalty "lecture" from one of the senior managers today. I'm surprised he sat down all of you young folks and talked about being loyal to the company. I guess they are spooked because they just lost Rob and a couple of your other co-workers to the competition.

When I started at Bloomfield, the management was very proud of the fact they had never had a layoff. They went through a few recessions and the partners toughed it out (sure they fired bad employees, but they never let anyone go just for economic reasons). I thought that was nice, but at the same time I was hearing the stories of my father-in-law who was regularly laid off as a normal part of a career in the construction industry.

Chainsaw Al Dunlap was also popular at the time. He was a CEO who would come into a company and "right-size" it by slashing personnel. And in the '80's, Jack Welch of GE was buying up companies and merging them with other GE businesses. They called him "Neutron" Jack for firing all the employees and leaving nothing but the buildings.

There was an engineer at Bloomfield who was close to retirement by the time I was hired. It was said he was very sharp and had always worked long hours. He rose to be a vice-president and had his heart set on being president of the company. Unfortunately for him, the CEO had a different idea and selected another vice-president to become president. That passed over vice-president immediately started tapering off his long work hours.

Since I am one who works hard and sets big goals for myself, this got me thinking about working for a large firm. It seemed wrong to set the thirty year goal of becoming president only to be passed over in year 29. What options would I have then?

Even though Bloomfield said they were loyal to me, I decided I wasn't going to spend my career there. I wanted more personal control over my career path. Even though I loved my boss, was working on challenging projects, and was being paid fairly – I decided to leave after about three years when an exciting opportunity came up with another company.

I had made the very important decision that I wasn't going to be blindly loyal to any company. Yes, your employer deserves an honest day's work for an honest wage and I always gave my very best. But I chose to do my very best because I was raised to work hard and I knew I would reap the most reward from my hard work.

Interestingly, it turns out Bloomfield had to change its mind too. They had to go through a few rounds of layoffs in the "Great Recession" of 2008 and 2009. One engineer I knew was laid off after thirty years. He was a loyal company man and had expected to retire from Bloomfield. I can't imagine being in that position.

There is one area where I am loyal though - with people. I am fiercely loyal to the people in my network. I try to help people find a job when they are looking for a change. I also refer work to people within my network whenever possible. This is an insurance policy for me. I figure if I am helpful to enough people, someday if I am in need, I'll get a helping hand back. It may not even be from someone I have helped, but I believe in the old cliché - what goes around comes around.

Be loyal to people, not necessarily companies.

Uncle Mike

Mike Smith • White Owl Consulting • 612-555-5550
100 Main St, #310, Minneapolis, MN 55411 • www.WhiteOwlConsulting.com

From: msmith@whiteowlconsulting.com
Sent: Saturday, July 9, 2011 8:03 AM
To: cdoe@acme-associates.com
Subject: **Small Talk**

Chris,
We missed you at the 4th of July picnic.

I feel your pain about the luncheon. I have been to plenty of them where the conversation just died at the table. It's always awkward.

Julie, an acquaintance of mine, is an exceptional conversationalist. Everyone feels better after they have chatted with her. I have heard that said about Bill Clinton and several other presidents too. They have a way of lighting up a room. What makes these people so good at conversation? Larry King, one of the best interviewers around, gives a few pointers in his book *How to Talk to Anyone, Anytime, Anywhere*, but he really boils it down to listening.

Julie is a great listener. She leans in and is enthusiastic. Julie totally focuses on you. I'm not sure she would turn away if the window broke next to her if you were in the middle of a sentence. You really know she cares because she asks great follow-up questions. A thirty second question will send you off talking for another five minutes. Key to showing this level of interest is realizing that everyone is an expert in something. Everyone has something they can teach you.

I am not a motorcycle aficionado. I didn't grow up working on cars or bikes and I never got into watching racing. One of my best friends has taught me a tremendous amount about racing and motorcycles. Chuck likes to talk about his races and I like to hear about them even though I probably wouldn't care much about racing if I hadn't met him.

So the key to being a great conversationalist has very little to do about you talking. It's mostly about you listening and questioning. Dale Carnegie pointed this out a hundred years ago and it's still true. Here are some tips for being a good conversationalist at the next awkward luncheon you attend:
- Homework - read general topic newspapers, blogs, magazines, or websites so you have some knowledge in a broad range of topics.

- Get people talking and keep them talking.
- When there is a lull in the conversation, here are some topics to keep things going. (Your follow-up questions will make or break the conversation.) - Where did they grow up? What schools did they go to? Have they been on any interesting trips? What kind of work do they do? What is their favorite hobby? Ask about the speaker, industry, speaking topic, etc.
- Ask emotional, how did you feel/what was it like questions as much as possible. Get away from questions that can be answered with one word.
- Get the whole group talking with a "what if" question, i.e. - What will happen to our industry if the banking industry collapses?

Stay away from religion and politics with acquaintances. Save those discussions for your close friends. Even if you think you know someone's beliefs you could end up being unpleasantly surprised. You would hate to offend a potential client or employer.

Lastly, you are much better off focusing on one or two people than trying to say hi to 100 people. Most people won't remember you if you are running around shaking hands. You have the best chance to make a great impression if you have a fifteen minute conversation with one person.

Work to stay informed and interested in those around you.

Uncle Mike

Mike Smith ● White Owl Consulting ● 612-555-5550
100 Main St, #310, Minneapolis, MN 55411 ● www.WhiteOwlConsulting.com

From: msmith@whiteowlconsulting.com
Sent: Tuesday, July 26, 2011 4:43 PM
To: cdoe@acme-associates.com
Subject: **Running a Meeting**

Chris,

So, Mr. Big Shot is running a meeting solo - good deal. It shows you are progressing in your career. You have sat in on several terrible meetings so you know what you don't want. No rambling affairs where you find yourself day dreaming. The type of meeting where everyone says great job at the end (mostly because the torture has stopped), even though nothing was accomplished. I am glad you care enough that you want to run an effective meeting.

There should be an objective for every meeting. Either you are telling people something, gaining agreement, or working to solve a problem. Those are about the only valid reasons to hold a meeting. Maybe the goal is to come up with five ways to deal with problem "x". Or, we have scenario "y" and need to figure out how to react. If you are just having a meeting to bring everyone up to speed, send an email instead.

The first artful point of running a meeting is figuring out how to not have the meeting. Can you accomplish your objective by bouncing emails back and forth? Maybe it is a topic that needs some give and take from a group - phone or video conference?

Emails are great for getting a specific question answered by one person. They are also a good way to keep people in the loop on a topic by copying them on the discussion. Phone and video conferences are meetings, so they need to follow the rules I am going to lay out. The big advantage with phone and video conferences is that they are usually a lot shorter and you don't have the inefficiency of travel. The down side to these meetings is that you don't get the body language and true collaboration of a face to face meeting. People can also be easily distracted (i.e., by playing solitaire, doing other work, etc.) without you knowing it.

There are times when you should sit down face to face for a meeting. Negotiations are best done in person so you can read the other side's body language. In person meetings can also help you build rapport with the people you are meeting with (as long as they are well run). So here is what to do if you decide a face to face meeting is the best way to go:

1. Get it scheduled as far in advance as possible.
2. Prepare an agenda for the meeting. It should include: the time and location of the meeting, the purpose of the meeting (one sentence objective), the items that will be discussed, and time limits for each item. The first two items of the agenda should be introductions of the meeting participants and review/revision of the agenda. Make sure you quickly get to the important parts of the agenda. Some people leave the important decisions to the end of the meeting and they get rushed through. Big mistake. Prioritize your agenda putting the most important topics first.
3. Email the agenda to the participants the day before the meeting. This will be a reminder for the meeting plus it will give them a chance to prepare.
4. Follow your agenda. Make sure you start and end on time, which will require you to be forceful in staying on task. At the end of the meeting, review the decisions that were made and who has follow-up tasks to do after the meeting.
5. Remember to follow-up with good minutes.

The best meetings include all the stakeholders, arrive at consensus, and are over quickly.

Uncle Mike

Mike Smith ● White Owl Consulting ● 612-555-5550
100 Main St, #310, Minneapolis, MN 55411 ● www.WhiteOwlConsulting.com

From: msmith@whiteowlconsulting.com
Sent: Sunday, August 14, 2011 8:59 PM
To: cdoe@acme-associates.com
Subject: **Business Travel**

Chris,
We had dinner with your folks last night. The weather was perfect for grilling and eating on the deck. You mom told me you are getting serious with your new girlfriend Christy. Don't let your mom put any pressure on you, but your folks seem to really like her.

Your dad told me you are going on your first business trip. Very heady stuff. I had a meeting in San Antonio, TX some years ago. It was my first out of state travel for a real meeting (I had only been to conventions out of state at that point). The meeting in San Antonio was part of a trade show get together and I was giving a little presentation, so I flew down early the morning of my meeting. I had a room at a nice hotel on the River Walk where the meeting was being held. Then I caught a flight back home early the next morning.

I could see the Alamo from my hotel window, but it was closed by the time I got out of my meeting. I ate better Tex Mex for dinner than I could have gotten at home, but other than that, it really didn't matter that I was in Texas. My meeting could have been in Siberia and I would have had about the same experience.

Business travel seems glamorous until you start doing it. You'll quickly realize how much work it is. I consider every hour away from my family as work. Based on discussions with my friends who travel, everyone eventually views business travel as work and doesn't see it as much of a perk.

I recommend you treat your trips as work. Bring work related reading to the airport. Plan memos and analysis you can do on your laptop. If you have to get a rental car, get an audiobook to listen to. Get room service breakfast to save yourself time. Work in your room. Try to get in some exercise. It will help you sleep better. Make sure you have internet access and do a bunch of emailing. Take care of administrative work. Don't burn time in a Starbucks (unless you're working) or by eating at an Applebee's. Definitely don't hit the bars. If you don't care about food, do room service. If you are a foodie, plan your dinners at local restaurants. It's the best way to experience the town in a short amount of time. View sightseeing as a bonus. Don't count on it.

Plan ahead so you can be productive while you travel.

Uncle Mike

p.s. Make sure you understand your company's travel policies and what is considered "normal." You don't want to raise eyebrows by staying in too nice a hotel or submitting a request to be reimbursed for a $300 meal at a steakhouse.

Mike Smith ● White Owl Consulting ● 612-555-5550
100 Main St, #310, Minneapolis, MN 55411 ● www.WhiteOwlConsulting.com

From: msmith@whiteowlconsulting.com
Sent: Tuesday, August 30, 2011 2:55 PM
To: cdoe@acme-associates.com
Subject: **The Late Person**

Chris,

Ugh! I just got back from a meeting where one of the guys was 25 minutes late. He didn't really apologize for being late and he didn't seem to have a good reason for not being on time. His office was three miles away from the meeting!

I became friends with a guy named Jack who is a professional, motivational speaker. I saw him speak for the first time when I was a sophomore in college. He told the story about how he used to be a late person. He was late to everything. We aren't talking about being a minute or two late. He was routinely 30 to 40 minutes late. One of his buddies called him on it. He asked Jack if he realized he was always late and that it pissed him off. Jack tried to downplay his late habit. He didn't think it was a big deal that he was late. I'm not sure how, but his buddy got through to him that it was very rude to be late. Being late sends the message that you see the other person's time as being of little value.

From that point on, Jack pledged to be an on time person. Of course he might get stuck in unforeseen traffic or have an emergency, but he is no longer a chronically late person. I have never been a late person in my life. I wasn't brought up that way. But Jack's speech still got through to me how important it is to be on time.

As a professional, you need to take this to heart. You should plan on being fifteen minutes early to every appointment. Hopefully this is enough of a cushion so you'll still be on time if you do hit an unforeseen traffic jam. If you are driving a long way or live in Los Angeles, you may need a bigger cushion. If it is a meeting in your own building, obviously 5 minutes is enough of a cushion. The important thing is to respect people's time.

The flip side of this respect is that even though you may show up fifteen minutes early, you don't call for the person until a couple of minutes before your meeting. Anything sooner than five minutes is rude in the other direction.

Now there are some people who are going to say it is a waste of time to sit idle for ten to fifteen minutes before every appointment. I agree - don't waste that time! There are two powerful things you can do with this extra time. One - if the meeting is at a company where you know other people, it is a good time to stop in and say hi. Most people appreciate a quick hello and it is a good excuse to stay current with the people in your network. Two - always bring along reading materials. Save your trade journals and other general reading for these moments. Make sure you always have something useful to read with you whenever you leave the office. It also never hurts to run through the meeting in your head while you are sitting in the lobby. Don't "invest" your time reading the People magazine the receptionist left on the lobby table.

Be an early person prepared to take advantage of the extra ten minutes.

Uncle Mike

Mike Smith • White Owl Consulting • 612-555-5550
100 Main St, #310, Minneapolis, MN 55411 • www.WhiteOwlConsulting.com

From: msmith@whiteowlconsulting.com
Sent: Thursday, September 15, 2011 9:25 PM
To: cdoe@acme-associates.com
Subject: **Strategy versus Execution**

Chris,

Take a breath and two steps back. I think you are shooting for perfection. Do you need perfection on this? Check in with your boss. She seems to be a huge improvement over your first boss (can you believe you have been working with her for a year already?). She'll give you good advice.

When I started at Bloomfield, my division head was named Louie Jackson. He was a very genial guy, but he could be feisty when he felt he had to be. Most of the new engineers in the company started in his division. Louie had about forty years on the job and had developed a few truisms that he beat into all of our heads. The one that has stuck with me the most is to get your design to 95% and then get it out for construction. This means you might miss a little detail here or there but nothing catastrophic. The field guys inspecting and surveying the project adjust for those things. Louie told me if you spend 100 hours to get to 95%, you are going to spend another 100 hours getting to 99% and it's impossible to get to 100%. Another boss of mine told me there comes a point in every project where you have to just shoot the engineer and build the thing.

I didn't write a formal business plan for my company. I thought about my potential customers and worked through my cash flow, but I didn't spend hundreds of hours writing a plan. Neither did any of the other half dozen people I know who have started successful companies. I do know about ten people who wrote really elaborate business plans. The interesting thing is that none of them were successful. One of the companies survived, but it looks nothing like the business plan.

Why bring this up? You aren't at the stage to be starting your own company yet. You're still in learning mode. I am bringing this up because I want you to be a doer. My experience has strongly taught me that you are better off implementing 100% of an 80% correct plan than implementing 80% of a 100% correct plan. A lot of it has to do with the fallacy of the 100% plan. Nothing is ever perfect.

The successful method involves rough planning, then implementing, then adjusting. In real life, plans are almost always iterative. The people who get hung up with staying on the perfect plan never get there. The real world looks a lot more like a pinball machine than a bowling lane. You do a lot of bouncing around to get from point A to point B, it isn't a straight line.

Get it to 95% and get it out the door!

Uncle Mike

Mike Smith • White Owl Consulting • 612-555-5550
100 Main St, #310, Minneapolis, MN 55411 • www.WhiteOwlConsulting.com

From: msmith@whiteowlconsulting.com
Sent: Monday, September 26, 2011 7:42 AM
To: cdoe@acme-associates.com
Subject: **Networking**

Chris,

It was good seeing you and Christy at the birthday party yesterday. Your Aunt Sara and I enjoyed meeting her. I was interested to hear why you think your co-worker Quiet Emma was passed over for the promotion. It isn't a surprise that Outgoing Steve got the promotion instead of Quiet Emma. It gets back to the proverbial idea of it's who you know not what you know. You joined Toastmasters. You are also on Facebook. Do you use LinkedIn? Networking is simple, yet your ability to do it will set your career on a much higher trajectory compared with your colleagues who don't do it.

Networking is like farming, not hunting. You plant seeds by making contacts. You water the seeds by staying in touch. You tend the crop consistently and eventually reap your harvest. Your entire network won't end up being productive, but like your crops, you don't know beforehand what will blossom and what will stagnate.

Here are the fields I want you to cultivate:

1. Stay in touch with your classmates. You aren't going to be able to tell who is going to be in a position of prominence twenty years from now. There will be natural ways to stay in touch - happy hours, reunions, etc. It is easy to lose track of most of your classmates, but stay in touch with your buddies and those in your area (your specialty or your geography).

2. Be a good colleague. Be a dependable and likeable person in the office. You might also want to play in the company basketball league or some other extra-curricular with your co-workers (just remember not to become best friends with people and don't be a drunk). It is amazing how quickly your coworkers will spread out in the industry. Many of the big law firms and consulting firms cultivate their own alumni groups! When somebody you know leaves a company, send them a congratulations note. Then stay in touch with them.

3. If you work with people outside of the company, get to know them. Stay in touch with the powerbrokers in your industry.

Also try to meet the people your own age. They are the powerbrokers of the future. Your network will mature with you.

4. You are active in your professional society. Make sure you are staying active on your committee. Working in committees with other people is the next best thing to working with them in your company. You get to prove you are likeable and dependable. These are great places to lay the foundation for your next job. As I said in number 2 above, stay in touch with people as they fan out.

5. Meet people at luncheons or classes. Find some common ground and make friends.

6. Cold call people you want to get to know (it's better to warm call by getting an introduction from someone you know – but either way you have to take the initiative to meet these people).

In the beginning of your career, you should focus on ideas one through four. I want you to stay organized and keep your contact database current. Make sure this database is a personal one that your company can't mine if you decide to leave the company.

Start farming!

Uncle Mike

Mike Smith ● White Owl Consulting ● 612-555-5550
100 Main St, #310, Minneapolis, MN 55411 ● www.WhiteOwlConsulting.com

From: msmith@whiteowlconsulting.com
Sent: Tuesday, September 27, 2011 4:59 PM
To: cdoe@acme-associates.com
Subject: **Re: Networking**

Chris,

Good question. I listed the where/who part of the equation for you, but you are right – I didn't say much about how to network. It is important to touch base with your contacts four to six times a year so they remember you when they need something you can help them with.

The how part is pretty simple. Find out what kinds of things would be helpful or interesting to the people in your network. If you come across something online, in a trade journal, at a lecture, an idea hits you in the shower - call them or drop them an email and let them know. If you want to be a little old fashioned, clip an article and mail it to them with a note. If you hear Tim Johnston left X, Y, Z and Associates, call Mary Clark over there to confirm and chat. Send out Fourth of July cards to your network. You'll get a few back from people who moved without you knowing. Track them down. Mailings are a good quality control check to keep your database up to date.

Most important - get on the phone immediately if you come up with a way to help someone. This should be an explicit part of getting to know people. Find out what helps them. If I'm working with a land developer, I find out what kind of property they like to buy so if I ever come across that situation I can connect them with the seller. This is all simple, but hard to implement - it all boils down to being thoughtful.

The jury is still out on how much business gets accomplished through things like LinkedIn. You need to do those things, but don't spend ten hours a week on your profile and think you are accomplishing great things.

Lastly, try to grab breakfast, coffee, lunch, or dinner with your contacts. Sharing a meal is an important way to develop a relationship in our culture. Don't be overt about this, but try to pick up the tab if you can. Dr. Robert Cialdini talks a lot about the obligation of reciprocity in his great book, *Influence: The Psychology of Persuasion*. He talks about how the Disabled Veterans give out paper flowers as do the Hari

Krishnas. Or the Cancer Society mails personalized return address labels to potential donors. These little gifts, even if you strongly don't want them, develop a psychological situation where you feel obligated to reciprocate. On top of that (even if you don't pick up the tab) it is easier to relax and get to know someone while breaking bread.

Make some calls and take a contact to lunch.

Uncle Mike

p.s. Do you and Christy have plans for this Saturday? Your Aunt Sara and I have Gopher football tickets for the game against Michigan, but we can't make it. It is supposed to be a perfect fall day. The tickets are yours if you can go. Let me know.

Mike Smith ● White Owl Consulting ● 612-555-5550
100 Main St, #310, Minneapolis, MN 55411 ● www.WhiteOwlConsulting.com

From: msmith@whiteowlconsulting.com
Sent: Friday, October 14, 2011 8:10 AM
To: cdoe@acme-associates.com
Subject: **Mentors**

Chris,

I'm very glad you come to me for advice. I love our emails and our chats. But you're starting to bounce industry specific stuff off me. While I'm happy to give you my opinion, it's time you also try to find a few other mentors who are directly in your field. Getting multiple points of view, even if they sometimes conflict, will help you broaden your perspective.

My very first boss, John, is still a close friend of mine many years after I left to take another job. When I told him I was leaving, first he swore at me (in good humor). Then we chatted about my new opportunity. Finally, he gave me a hug and congratulated me. As I turned around to leave his office, he kicked me in the rear end and called me names. That's the kind of guy he is.

I try to see him ten to twelve times a year, mostly because I like seeing him. At this point it's easy to justify because he is also one of my best clients (he was my very first client and remains in my top five). He has given me a lot of great advice, including encouraging me to go after that City of Riverside staff job I landed even though I didn't meet the advertised qualifications.

My wish is that you can find yourself an industry coach like John. In the ideal world you will find several. I have four gray haired guys I meet with individually at least once a year. They are my sounding board. I worked to find people with different backgrounds and experiences so I have a diverse group of people I can talk to. They have two things in common: (1) they have more battle scars than I have and (2) they are willing to share what they learned from getting those scars.

Your potential mentors are going to come out of your network. Think about the people you have met at professional society meetings. Is there something about them or their career that you can learn from? Then contact them to let them know you would like to use them as a resource.

A secondary network of mentors is authors and bloggers. Some of my mentors are Dale Carnegie, Jeffrey Gitomer, Robert Cialdini, Seth Godin, Peter Block, Ford Harding, Tom Peters, Guy Kawasaki, Bob Sutton, Harry Beckwith, Jeffrey Fox, Stephen Covey, Benjamin Franklin, Abraham Lincoln, and Garr Reynolds. I have never met any of them (especially Franklin and Lincoln), yet they are right up there with John in influencing my career. I hope you'll make time to read some of these folks' advice. There are probably other authors you'll find helpful too.

A third place to look for advice is SCORE. They are a group of retirees who will mentor you on any business topic for free. SCORE members have helped me quite a bit, especially with starting my own business. I have talked and emailed with four or five SCORE volunteers as I have faced different business challenges. Keep them in mind. Go to score.org if you ever consider starting a business.

Mentors help you get outside your own biases to see other opinions and options. They are an invaluable resource.

Make developing your own mentor network a high priority.

Uncle Mike

Mike Smith • White Owl Consulting • 612-555-5550
100 Main St, #310, Minneapolis, MN 55411 • www.WhiteOwlConsulting.com

From: msmith@whiteowlconsulting.com
Sent: Wednesday, October 26, 2011 5:19 PM
To: cdoe@acme-associates.com
Subject: **The Art of the Note**

Chris,

You're welcome! I enjoyed getting the thank you note you sent and I'm glad to see your Mom's lessons are sticking with you. Writing thank you notes is both good manners and good business. I read that Ronald Reagan wrote tens of thousands of notes in his life and I've also heard a lot of other presidents have been prolific note writers. Eleanor Roosevelt even wrote thank you notes for thank you notes. I am not sure if President Obama is big into handwriting notes, but there was a lot of press about him texting and emailing extensively during his campaign.

The handwritten note was a dying art form when I started my career and it is nearly extinct today with email and text messaging. This lack of handwritten notes is good news for you because it presents a way to differentiate yourself. Get yourself some good, blank note cards. Don't buy the ones with the cheesy Thank You swooping across the front because you should send more than just thank you notes. Hopefully your company provides note cards with the company logo on them. You can even go out and buy some postcards if you want.

Here are some reasons to send out a note:
- You were just interviewed - say thank you.
- You were just hired by a company - say thank you.
- You were just turned down for a job - thank them for the opportunity.
- You met someone - send a follow-up note saying you enjoyed meeting them.
- You just finished a project - say thank you.
- You were just selected to work on a project - say thank you.
- You were just turned down for a project - thank them for the opportunity.
- You got a raise - say thank you.
- Someone you know got a promotion or new job - say congratulations.
- You read a book or article you liked - let the author know. Especially if you know the author.

- Someone you know just landed a good project or did something good - say congratulations.
- You read something one of your contacts would like - clip it out or print it out and send it them saying you thought the article would interest them.
- You discovered something that could benefit one of your contacts (i.e. an accountant who finds a new deduction) - let them know.
- Somebody did something you appreciated, anything - say thank you!
- A contact's birthday.
- Congratulate someone on their retirement.
- A contact has a child.
- A condolence for a death in a contact's family.
- A get well card.

Besides all the reasons above, as a business owner, I also send out a thank you note every time we receive payment for a project. Trust me - I'm happy to get paid! But this is also a small way to differentiate myself. I know it worked a couple years ago when I met an out of town client for the first time. I had been working for him for several months on a study and had written a few thank you notes for paid invoices. When we were introduced by an intermediary at a big project meeting, he shook my hand and said, "You're the thank you note guy!" Differentiate yourself!

Thanks for the thank you note.

Uncle Mike

Mike Smith ● White Owl Consulting ● 612-555-5550
100 Main St, #310, Minneapolis, MN 55411 ● www.WhiteOwlConsulting.com

From: msmith@whiteowlconsulting.com
Sent: Saturday, November 5, 2011 1:32 PM
To: cdoe@acme-associates.com
Subject: **Your Brain and Your Body**

Chris,

I can't believe we are getting snow this early in November. This is bad for our road construction projects. We were hoping to have until Thanksgiving to wrap them up.

So you're addicted to Red Bull and coffee. You aren't doing yourself any favors in the long run. There are other things you can do to keep your energy levels up (and learn how to work around the periods when your energy is down). Trust me. I have had my own issues with coffee.

I recently read *Brain Rules*, by Dr. John Medina. He strongly states that our brains work better when our bodies are moving. He even goes so far as to say the modern cube is about the worst environment imaginable for brain activity. It seems humans evolved to think best while we are moving and doing physical activity. This should matter a lot to you since you are making a living with your brain.

There are some crazy ideas like walking desks (you walk on a treadmill) or standing desks, but here are some mainstream ideas you can implement without looking like a fool:

- Get out of the office to take walks. Your grandma got in the habit of walking for thirty minutes over her lunch hour and she loved it. She walked with a group of co-workers and sometimes their walks morphed into walking meetings.
- Get out of your chair regularly.
- Sit on a physioball instead of a chair. A lot of offices have at least one person who is doing this. You probably don't want to be the first one doing this though.
- Understand circadian rhythms – your body's natural clock. There is science that backs up the siesta concept. Most people's brains slow down in the mid-afternoon. Schedule your day so your least demanding work happens then. Never schedule an important meeting mid-afternoon and never give a speech in the middle of the afternoon!

- Sleep is radically important. Get the 7 to 9 hours your body tells you it needs.
- Lift weights and get cardiovascular exercise. The research shows your brain makes more neural connections if you exercise regularly. You get smarter.

When I was in college, I worked on and off at a distribution company picking orders and boxing them up. I enjoyed college a lot and still had some maturing to do. I went into work one morning hung over. My boss had no sympathy and worked me extra hard. I never made that mistake again and it almost goes without saying – don't overindulge during the workweek.

Work with your brain not against it.

Uncle Mike

Mike Smith ● White Owl Consulting ● 612-555-5550
100 Main St, #310, Minneapolis, MN 55411 ● www.WhiteOwlConsulting.com

From: msmith@whiteowlconsulting.com
Sent: Tuesday, November 15, 2011 4:39 PM
To: cdoe@acme-associates.com
Subject: **Good to see you....**

Chris,
Sorry to hear the luncheon was boring. Not all of them are interesting, but it is important for you to be a regular. Hopefully you met a person or two you can add to your network.

Funny that you bumped into that guy from your high school but not so funny that you couldn't remember his name. We've all been there. You bump into an acquaintance. They seem happy to see you. For god's sake, they remember your name. Unfortunately, you can place them, but you still can't come up with their name. Trying harder pushes their name further away from you. I always try to smile a lot and muddle through the conversation without admitting I forgot their name. Certainly not the best practice.

Dale Carnegie wrote in his 1936 classic *How to Win Friends and Influence People* that the sweetest words a person can hear is their own name. It's true. You honor someone by remembering their name. You are saying they are important enough for you to remember them.

Its work to remember people's names, but doing so will definitely help you in your career. Here are some tips for getting names stuck in your brain.

- When you shake someone's hand look at their face and repeat their name. Look for unique facial features. Hone in on one thing. Do they have a mole? A dimple? Vibrant eyes? Bald? Big ears? It doesn't matter. Just pick one thing to focus on. Now imagine their name written out next to that feature.
- Use the person's name as much as you can in the conversation without being obnoxious. Repetition will help ingrain and they will like hearing their name.
- If they have a name that could be spelled different ways or it is a unique name, ask them to spell it. People won't mind. Actually they will be flattered you care.
- Visualize them with someone you know who has the same name. It's helpful to pick one Mike, Tim, Kaitlyn, etc. that you know

and always use them as your reference. My brother-in-law Ted is my match for any Teds I meet.

- After you meet a business contact, read through their business card later that day. Visualize them. Jot a few notes about your conversation on the back of the card. It is especially helpful to review the notes on the back of your cards before you have a meeting. If you are going to Carlson Companies, go through all of your contacts at Carlson Companies just in case you bump into them. You'll blow someone's mind if you say - your daughter Janie must be about 8 now. Is she in second grade?
- Back to the notes - write them a note that day or the next. The review helps.
- Try to link their name to an image. John Doe is pretty easy. Think Bambi. One of my favorites is a couple of images I came up for my co-worker Linda Colhagen. I thought of a dirty coalminer eating a pint of Hagen-Dazs ice cream.

Remembering people's names will pay off in the long run.

Uncle Mike

Mike Smith ● White Owl Consulting ● 612-555-5550
100 Main St, #310, Minneapolis, MN 55411 ● www.WhiteOwlConsulting.com

From: msmith@whiteowlconsulting.com
Sent: Friday, November 25, 2011 9:19 AM
To: cdoe@acme-associates.com
Subject: **Get Some Audiobooks**

Chris,
We missed you yesterday at Thanksgiving. I hope you had a good time meeting Christy's family. Your mom tells me your commute is driving you crazy and no - even though I'm a traffic engineer I can't help you zip past everyone.

Somehow humans are wired to have about a maximum of a twenty minute commute. This has been true since the time of the industrial revolution when families moved within about a mile and a half of the factory (about a twenty minute walk away). As trolleys came along people lived further away from work. Now we have the automobile, but people may choose to live downtown and walk to work or take transit in. In any event, I'm guessing you spend 30 to 60 minutes a day getting to and from work.

You probably listen to an iPOD or your radio in your car. Not terrible, but it is the equivalent of being a couch potato. You should engage your mind. Get yourself a library card if you don't have one. Go to the library website and reserve an audiobook. They'll email you when you can pick it up. Listen to it while you are commuting, and if you picked a decent one, you'll get hooked.

I suggest starting with a thriller like a John Grisham, Michael Crichton or John Sanford book. Make sure it is read by a professional actor. You'll find yourself excited about your commute so you can keep going on the story. It really helps smooth out your attitude if you get stuck in a traffic jam because you are doing something enjoyable while you're stuck.

After you are hooked on the concept (and trust me, you will be), you can put on your halo and start listening to non-fiction books. Hopefully you'll learn something. Warning - a fair amount of non-fiction can get boring. Usually the author reads the book themselves. You'll learn to appreciate books read by trained actors. Make sure you mix up the types of audiobooks you are listening to so you don't get bored.

My friend Rick has a commute that usually takes more than an hour and can take hours if we get a bad snowstorm. He is addicted to audiobooks. Rick and his wife have taken the cool step of turning it into a book club. At least once a month she reads one of the books he is listening to. It gives them something to chat about.

Of course you can do the variation of downloading podcasts or audiobooks (the new stuff usually costs something) if you don't want to go to the library. But the library is free and it will probably force you to branch out in different directions.

If you drive a lot for work (I occasionally drive to meetings three or four hours away) this is the only way to go if you find yourself outside of civilization with no radio stations you can tolerate. Being engrossed in an audiobook will keep you from getting drowsy too.

Make your car your University on wheels.

Uncle Mike

Mike Smith ● White Owl Consulting ● 612-555-5550
100 Main St, #310, Minneapolis; MN 55411 ● www.WhiteOwlConsulting.com

From: msmith@whiteowlconsulting.com
Sent: Thursday, December 1, 2011 5:59 PM
To: cdoe@acme-associates.com
Subject: **I'll get back to you**

Chris,
I got your voicemail. I'm in the middle of a tough project that's due tomorrow.

I'll call you tomorrow night.

Uncle Mike

Mike Smith • White Owl Consulting • 612-555-5550
100 Main St, #310, Minneapolis, MN 55411 • www.WhiteOwlConsulting.com

From: msmith@whiteowlconsulting.com
Sent: Monday, December 12, 2011 4:52 PM
To: cdoe@acme-associates.com
Subject: **Re: They Ignored My Recommendation**

Chris,
Welcome to my world! Your role as a professional is often to make recommendations, but you are not the implementer. Craft a reasonable argument and try to guide your client or your boss, but at the end of the day, the decision is out of your hands. They get to choose if they want to take your advice or not.

Will, my boss at Riverside burned this lesson into my brain. A few weeks into the job, the mayor came in and said he wanted a stop sign installed at an intersection. I was in the meeting and Will explained to the mayor the pros and cons of putting in the stop sign. I chimed in with all of the reasons it wasn't a good decision to install the stop sign (unnecessary delays, potentially more crashes, disrespect for the stop sign since it wasn't really needed, etc.). I was the traffic engineer. I felt I was hired to make these decisions.

Will told the mayor we'd get the stop signs installed in a week. I was pretty upset. Why was I hired if not to make these decisions? After the mayor left, Will explained the mayor could have us fired. The mayor was under political pressure from his constituents and had a lot invested in this decision on the other side.

Will explained we were there to advise the mayor and city council, but ultimately they were elected to run the city. He pointed out the political nature of our situation. He also pointed out that the stop sign was a marginally bad idea, not a horribly bad idea. He had survived twenty years as a city engineer through multiple mayoral regimes because of his political savvy. Ultimately, I needed to learn to pick which battles were worth fighting. I also needed to learn that in many situations I am an advisor. To stay sane, I learned to divorce myself from the outcome after I gave my advice.

I am not telling you to give bad advice. Do thorough research. Examine the alternatives. Make a clear recommendation and document it. Point out (in a politically correct fashion) if you think your boss or client is making a catastrophic decision. This is what you are being paid to do.

But then you need to let the chips fall where they may and keep your sanity.

Pick your battles.

Uncle Mike

p.s. How was the company party Saturday? What did Christy think? Was your CEO longwinded again?

Mike Smith • White Owl Consulting • 612-555-5550
100 Main St, #310, Minneapolis, MN 55411 • www.WhiteOwlConsulting.com

From: msmith@whiteowlconsulting.com
Sent: Friday, January 6, 2012 4:29 PM
To: cdoe@acme-associates.com
Subject: **Barry the Backstabber**

Chris,
Are you really going ice fishing? The news is predicting a snowstorm.

Ouch. I was really hoping Acme didn't have a "Barry the Backstabber." These are guys who take credit for your work. They are always trying to gain points without doing work. This involves trying to rip down their co-workers so they can prop themselves up. Barry the Backstabber is usually a big gossip.

You need to neutralize Barry the Backstabber so he can never get you again. Your first defense is just to stay away from him. Keep your encounters brief and businesslike. Do not chat with him in the hallway. Never leave your back exposed to his knife.

Next, you need to stand up for yourself. You'll need to be proactive whenever you are in a meeting with Barry or are working on the same project. Stand up and explain your work. Be clear about your contribution. Don't give him an opening to steal your thunder. Dance around him as much as possible so you don't have very much direct contact. Let other people be his target.

Luckily, Barry the Backstabber is not your boss. You are in a terrible bind if you ever have a backstabber as a boss. You basically have to decide to live with the situation, try to go over their head, or leave. Often your best option is to find another job. Early in your career it is a losing proposition to go over your boss' head. Fairly or unfairly, most young people who complain a lot get labeled as rabble rousers by upper management and end up being black balled.

The best way to deal with a backstabber - never leave your back exposed.

Uncle Mike

Mike Smith • White Owl Consulting • 612-555-5550
100 Main St, #310, Minneapolis, MN 55411 • www.WhiteOwlConsulting.com

From: msmith@whiteowlconsulting.com
Sent: Monday, January 23, 2012 1:42 PM
To: cdoe@acme-associates.com
Subject: **Magic Words**

Chris,

I just got back from having lunch with a potential hire. We were just getting together to stay in touch. I don't think he realized I was evaluating him. I'm not sure if he was having a bad day, but he was awfully rude to the server at the restaurant. That certainly soured my opinion of him.

I hope you are continuing to practice what your parents taught you - how to be polite and pleasant. Being a well mannered person. Using words such as thank you, you're welcome, please, hello, excuse me, I'm sorry, etc. In our culture, these are magic words. Unless you are an attorney being paid to be a jerk (Ivan the Jerk), you should use these words as often as possible (Ivan the Jerk pretty much has to be rude to stay in character - at least during working hours).

Think of these words as the grease in the machine you call a life. Use the words at Starbucks. Use them at the gas station. Use them at home. Use them at work with both your co-workers and your boss. Use them with people who are handling your food (you have no idea what is happening to your burger behind the closed door). You'll be in a better frame of mind and it will improve the mood of those you come in contact with.

You should go a step further. Open doors for people. Buy thoughtful gifts. Be in a good mood. Be grateful. Remember to be sincere and to look sincere. A smile goes a long way when you are saying thank you or please.

Keep these simple, magical words in mind any time you are dealing with people and always do the right thing.

Uncle Mike

Mike Smith • White Owl Consulting • 612-555-5550
100 Main St, #310, Minneapolis, MN 55411 • www.WhiteOwlConsulting.com

From: msmith@whiteowlconsulting.com
Sent: Friday, February 10, 2012 4:51 PM
To: Chris@gmail.com
Subject: **Re: Getting back into the swing of things**

Chris,
I am glad you are feeling better. I still can't believe you got chicken pox. I had no idea it could be that serious, but I've never heard of an adult coming down with it either. I'm glad Christy took you to the hospital right away. It was obviously serious since they kept you there for a week. Look on the bright side, you can do something low key for Valentine's Day next week.

Are you sure you should go back to work already? Call your boss Monday morning to talk through your schedule. I think you are going to need to go in for just a couple of hours for the first few days. You need to slowly build up your strength. The worst thing you can do is to push yourself too hard and end up back in the hospital.

You've been out for two weeks with this emergency, so you don't know what's going on with your projects. The first thing you should do is go through your to do list with your boss to find out the status of all of your tasks and projects. Hopefully your teammates picked up your work and were able to cover for you. You can't physically put in long hours to try to catch up.

Work with your boss to prioritize a new to do list. You need to get through the urgent items first. Lay out your schedule assuming you are working limited hours your first week back. Also assume you are only going to be about fifty percent as productive.

The same work rules apply, but are even more important. Eat right. Drink plenty of water. Move around about every forty-five minutes. Communicate clearly with your boss. Limit the caffeine. Get a good night's sleep. Do your most important work first thing. Don't get distracted with email and administrative work. Be intensely results oriented. Until you feel 100%, work short days instead of going out to lunch. This is also a good excuse to skip non-essential meetings.

Since your boss emailed out a notice to your contacts that you were out sick (she seems so much sharper than your last boss), you shouldn't have any urgent emails or voicemails. Honestly, I think you should wait a week before going through your emails. Wait until you get the urgent things done on your to do list. Think of yourself as being a nurse in an emergency room at the hospital. You need to take care of the critical patients first. The car crash victim comes before the person who is in with a cold.

When coming back from an illness, you need to focus like a laser beam on your urgent tasks.

Uncle Mike

Mike Smith ● White Owl Consulting ● 612-555-5550
100 Main St, #310, Minneapolis, MN 55411 ● www.WhiteOwlConsulting.com

From: msmith@whiteowlconsulting.com
Sent: Sunday, February 26, 2012 2:38 PM
To: cdoe@acme-associates.com
Subject: **Creativity**

Chris,
I think you are a little too close to the problem. I can "hear" your frustration in your email. Try to take a breather and you'll likely see a couple of solutions that aren't apparent right now.

I stopped by a client's office a few weeks ago to talk about one of their new projects. A city had their consultant prepare the traffic study for a large area soon to be developed. One of the companies developing part of the vacant land hired a civil engineering firm (my client) to start designing the site. This is typical. The civil engineer on the project asked me to stop by their office because he wanted me to review the city's traffic study as a quality control check. A few of the assumptions the city made about the area had changed slightly.

They gave me a stack of documents to review and we spent five minutes looking at the road designs. The development will have access from two tee intersections on a county road with a big vacant area on the other side of the road. I asked if the tee intersections will ultimately be upgraded to have four legs when the other side of the road develops. The civil engineer agreed it was a good question. Unfortunately, the land is in a different city and the county road is the boundary between the two cities. I definitely needed to dig into it further to make sure the plans provided the best solution.

I'm an engineer. A profession not exactly known for creativity. We typically think of artists when we think of creativity, not engineers or accountants. However we are all being paid to be creative. We need to think through all alternatives (no matter how off the wall), develop criteria to measure the alternatives, and then finally recommend one of the alternatives as the best fit for our criteria. We need to see all of the angles. Even though I am not "creative" I was able to see an angle a lot of people missed with that fourth leg.

When I am faced with a new problem, I tackle it in a systematic way that pushes me further than a typical brainstorming session. I boil the problem down to a phrase and write that at the top of the page. Then I force myself to come up with ten different ideas related to the problem. Then I take each of those ten related ideas and force myself to come up with five related sub-ideas under the prime ideas. I end up with something that looks like a family tree with the problem phrase at the top of the page. Push yourself further and develop more layers if it is a big problem.

Systematically push yourself when problem solving.

Uncle Mike

Mike Smith ● White Owl Consulting ● 612-555-5550
100 Main St, #310, Minneapolis, MN 55411 ● www.WhiteOwlConsulting.com

From: msmith@whiteowlconsulting.com
Sent: Monday, February 27, 2012 9:41 PM
To: cdoe@acme-associates.com
Subject: **Re: Creativity**

Chris,

I'm glad you're going through the "family tree" with your brainstorming. I think it will help push you to the right solution. To help prod me in my "family tree" brainstorming, I go through these questions to spark ideas:

- What are the things I truly know? What are my assumptions?
- What are my constraints (be honest – are these assumed constraints or known constraints)?
- What other information/data do I need to collect?
- Do we have to solve this problem – doing nothing or delaying the decision may be the best answer.
- Can I break the problem into steps to tackle one at a time?
- Define what a successful outcome looks like.
- What is the worst outcome that would be acceptable?
- Have others faced this problem? What did they do?

The last thing about creativity is to let the ideas sit in your subconscious if it all possible. Think through the problem over a course of days, not minutes. Everyone has had a Eureka moment where a solution pops into your head out of nowhere. They almost always come after a good night's sleep at a time when you aren't thinking about the problem at all.

My best ideas usually come to me when I am taking a shower in the morning. Give the supercomputer inside your skull a chance to work on the problem. Think about the problem on day one. Think about your criteria on day two. Think about alternatives on day three. Then work it out a few days later. You'll come up with a much better and more well thought out solution if you take the time.

Creativity brings solutions.

Uncle Mike

Mike Smith • White Owl Consulting • 612-555-5550
100 Main St, #310, Minneapolis, MN 55411 • www.WhiteOwlConsulting.com

From: msmith@whiteowlconsulting.com
Sent: Thursday, March 8, 2012 4:01 PM
To: cdoe@acme-associates.com
Subject: **Tim the Intern**

Chris,
Your Aunt Sara and I are looking forward to seeing you and Christy at your folks tomorrow.   Sara can't wait to see Christy's ring. Congratulations again on the engagement (you are carrying on a family tradition of marrying great women).

Being assigned an intern is a fantastic opportunity. Don't look at it as a burden. Tim the Intern will be nervous and excited as he starts. Be a good human being and help him out. The bonus is that he can be a real help to you since you have him for six months.

You had two good internships, so think back to what your bosses did for you. Work hard to give Tim a good experience. Here are some thoughts:
- Walk Tim the Intern around the building and introduce him to different departments. Explain what they do and why they do it. Teach him how the company makes money.
- Give him the big picture. Then break down how both of you fit into the big picture with what you do. Make him realize that everything he will be doing over the next six months matters. There is no busy work.
- Think through a six month plan for Tim the Intern that can grow his skills. Start him off with basic grunt work, but assign him a little more responsibility each week if you can.
- Try to build up Tim so he is producing valuable, independent work midway through his internship.
- Keep an open door (cube entrance) policy. You want him to come to you with anything that is on his mind. Not just work stuff. You have an opportunity to become a personal mentor with his schooling and career.
- Remember you are his boss though, not his buddy. Keep your relationship away from the personal. Don't go out drinking with him.
- Be a good manager – give the big picture. Break his project down into tasks. Develop a plan together. Give him benchmarks

for when he needs to check back in with you. Help him take baby steps.

- If he comes to work hung over, work him extra hard and keep him late. It will teach him a valuable lesson (and it is a little fun in a twisted way).
- Try to get him some work assignments with other people in the department or company midway into his internship. Let Tim the Intern experience how different people operate.

Make sure he gets a good experience that will help him land a full time job later. Maybe you'll see Tim the Intern is really talented and Acme should snap him up.

There is also some benefit here for you too. Working with an intern is a great practice run for when you will be managing your own staff. I bet you will also learn a few things by working with Tim. Teaching will make you sharper too.

We learn deepest by teaching others.

Uncle Mike

Mike Smith ● White Owl Consulting ● 612-555-5550
100 Main St, #310, Minneapolis, MN 55411 ● www.WhiteOwlConsulting.com

From: msmith@whiteowlconsulting.com
Sent: Tuesday, March 20, 2012 7:57 PM
To: cdoe@acme-associates.com
Subject: **Stress!**

Chris,

It sounds like you are stressed out with your deadline. You need to figure out how to deal with this (besides having a beer and watching the March Madness basketball games).

College should have prepared you pretty well for life as a professional. Every once in a while you have a project that makes you feel like it's finals week. A lot of folks feel more pressure on the job than in college. We view our jobs as pass/fail with failure really sucking.

You can go to Barnes & Noble and pick up hundreds of books that will tell you how to deal with stress. The best techniques, according to Dr. John Medina in *Brain Rules*, are ones that allow you to take back some control. Human beings are most stressed when we feel like we have no way of affecting the outcome. A lot of the same advice for beating procrastination applies to beating stress – break your tasks down into manageable steps.

Another way to deal with stress is to do something physical. Totally exhausting yourself is one way to manage the stress.

I left my secure government job with a one year consulting contract in hand at a manufacturing company. I was still running my own business, but I was working about thirty hours at the manufacturing plant. I packed up my family and moved about an hour and a half away from our family and friends. Seven months into the job, I realized it wasn't the kind of work I wanted to do and I didn't try to renew the contract (I am not sure if the owner would have renewed it or not). So here I am with a small business that can't pay my bills, living about an hour and a half away from the metropolitan area where I can get another job.

The first thing I did was order a driveway full of rock and landscaping plastic from my garden center. I hand graded the dirt around the entire house, put down the plastic, and spent three days shoveling rock around the house. I fixed the drainage problems we were having. It was hard work. I slept great. My mind worked through my options while I was physically working on something I could control. I came up with a game plan for my next career move and I built my business. I am pretty sure I wouldn't have done as well if I started scheming and worrying. The physical work got me over the hump of the most stressful situation I have been in. If you have stress in your life, part of the solution is to get active. If a huge stress hits, like losing your job, figure out a physical project that will exhaust you. The best ones involve a shovel and wheelbarrow.

Work to gain control over small areas of your destiny.

Uncle Mike

Mike Smith • White Owl Consulting • 612-555-5550
100 Main St, #310, Minneapolis, MN 55411 • www.WhiteOwlConsulting.com

From: msmith@whiteowlconsulting.com
Sent: Monday, April 2, 2012 7:43 AM
To: cdoe@acme-associates.com
Subject: **Face Time**

Chris,

Your Aunt Sara told me yesterday she was pregnant. After I stopped hyperventilating she told me she was joking. I think that was the best April Fool's joke that has ever been played on me.

That's great that your company is implementing a new flex time work schedule. I don't always need to be in my office to get things done. I often look in the mirror and give myself permission to work from a coffee shop. The people I work with also work outside of the office and we all like it this way. We have built up a level of trust on our team.

Currently, *Results Only Work Environment* is a hot topic. It's the idea, largely pioneered at Best Buy, that time doesn't matter, only results do. If you can work effectively via the internet for four weeks from Peru, your boss shouldn't care. They should be supportive and it shouldn't matter if you are in the office.

This can work, but it takes a top notch manager. Tasks need to be clearly defined. You need to have a clear picture of what the results are supposed to be and you have to have a clear deadline. There needs to be clear lines of communication - when you will/won't be available via email and cell phone. I say you need a good manager, because they can't run down the hall and switch your priorities on the fly. It won't work for those firefighter types who bounce from one raging fire to the next.

The results only issue is a sticky one if you are working in a company that essentially makes money by selling your time. It is a topic management needs to work out. A lot of companies do provide leeway in work hours. Most of them want you to put in your forty to fifty hours. They don't care if you start at 6 a.m. and leave at 4 p.m. or start at 9 a.m. and leave at 7 p.m. You may or may not need to sign in and out or fill out a timecard. While I physically punched a clock when I worked as a Teamster loading produce trucks, I haven't seen that in any of the agencies or companies I have been to over the course of my professional career.

Now there are two important questions you need to answer as a young professional, (1) what is the best way to become a competent professional and (2) what is the best way to advance your career. I don't think you should take your boss up on the offer to work from home every day. As part of your learning curve, you are going to have questions that are better answered in person. Email and cell phones can work for this type of stuff, but you won't go off on the educational tangents that happen when you are sitting in your boss' office. Also you aren't going to develop as large a network with your co-workers. Bumping into the other young professionals at the coffee pot, even if you don't work with them directly, will help you build rapport. And opportunities seem to pop up just by being there. For these reasons, I recommend you put in a fair amount of face time at the office.

When I started at Bloomfield, I quickly learned that a lot of the bigwigs worked in the office on the weekends. We were also expected to work 45 to 55 hours a week. I put in 8 to 9 hours a day Monday through Friday and I then would go in on Saturdays. I found there was a lot of chit chatting on Saturday mornings, so one weekend I decided to go in Sunday afternoon instead of Saturday so I could really concentrate.

As you'd expect, there weren't very many people there on Sunday. Most sane people take off at least one day a week. I was able to concentrate in the solitude and I got a lot done. I also bumped into several vice-presidents and the CEO in the hallways as I was coming and going. After that, I gravitated towards working on Sundays instead of Saturdays when I needed to work on the weekend. I think the high ups may have thought I was working Saturdays too. I developed a reputation as a hard worker and I know I caught the eye of upper management. Plus I was more efficient with the weekend time I put in.

When I worked for the City of Riverside there were guys who got in around 7:00 a.m. and left promptly at 4:30 p.m. Then there were others who got in at 8:00 a.m. and left at 5:00 p.m. Most days I got in at 7:30 and left at 4:45. The early folks thought I was part of their crowd and so did the late folks.

If you are going to have to put in long hours, think about management's perception. Like it or not, perception is part of the game. Try to get the biggest "perception" bang for your extra hours. When in doubt, try to be to your desk 15 minutes before your boss gets to work and leave 5 minutes after she does. You'll be perceived as a very hard worker.

Beware of another old cliché that's still true – out of sight/out of mind.

Uncle Mike

Mike Smith ● White Owl Consulting ● 612-555-5550
100 Main St, #310, Minneapolis, MN 55411 ● www.WhiteOwlConsulting.com

From: msmith@whiteowlconsulting.com
Sent: Saturday, April 14, 2012 8:02 AM
To: cdoe@acme-associates.com
Subject: **Who's Knocking?**

Chris,

Wow! So you're looking for that first house. I remember when your Aunt Sara and I started looking - exciting time. There is, however, something I want you to keep in mind.

A little company was in startup mode in California about 40 years ago. The founders decided it was time to hire an engineer as their first employee. They went through a standard interviewing process and they found the perfect candidate. He wasn't in California, but he said he'd consider moving. They started talking money. Since they were a start up, they couldn't offer much in the way of salary, but they could offer stock options. The guy talked to his wife. She wasn't too excited about packing up to take a job where the guy would make less money. They had a couple of kids and they were a couple of years into their mortgage. It just didn't feel right to them. The guy turned down the job offer.

On to candidate number two. They started talking to a young immigrant named Andy Grove. He was smart. He had a good education. He had saved up a little money. He thought working for a little company called Intel sounded like a good opportunity. He took the low salary and stock options. Mr. Grove built up Intel and retired as Chairman of the Board as a billionaire in 2004. I don't know what happened to the other guy, but I am guessing he wasn't a billionaire.

Sara and I had a similar experience, except we aren't billionaires (or millionaires - I am happy to report we are hundredaires). We have always been pretty frugal. It helped that we got married two weeks after I got my first job out of college. We started out with nothing and it was pretty easy to keep living the college lifestyle. We lived frugally while we paid off our school loans. Then we saved enough money to bootstrap starting our company as a moonlighting venture. A little while later we had enough money in the bank to leap into the company full time.

One of my mentors taught me early on that cash is king. It doesn't matter how much people owe you (your income) and it doesn't matter how much you are paying out (your bills). The secret to the formula is to make sure the cash is coming in a little faster than it is going out. I am not saying you should deprive yourself. But keep in mind that a huge mortgage or spending a lot on a credit card financed vacation aren't the best ideas.

Good rules of thumb for your budding financial life – put ten percent of your salary into retirement (401k), ten percent into a rainy day savings account, and don't spend more than thirty percent on your lodging. Automatic deduction plans are good for the rainy day savings account so you don't even think about it. Your company automatically withdraws your 401k. You can live on the rest. It never hurts your karma to give some money to charity too.

Maintain a manageable lifestyle so you are in a position to say yes when opportunity knocks.

Uncle Mike

Mike Smith ● White Owl Consulting ● 612-555-5550
100 Main St, #310, Minneapolis, MN 55411 ● www.WhiteOwlConsulting.com

From: msmith@whiteowlconsulting.com
Sent: Saturday, April 21, 2012 2:57 PM
To: cdoe@acme-associates.com
Subject: **Burn Out**

Chris,
I'm a little surprised you are questioning your career choice already, but I knew it would come at some point. Maybe you're just antsy because of the spring weather.

I know a fair number of people in my industry who started out their careers as engineers or planners and eventually moved to a different career. Some of them totally moved on, others went to work for developers managing projects. They got tired of the daily grind of being a professional with technical responsibilities. We are currently in a down economy and some of them have been laid off. They are trying to get back into engineering but are having a tough go of it because their skills are rusty.

It reminds me of the Law of Undulation which C.S. Lewis wrote about in *The Screwtape Letters*. The book follows the conversation between an elder demon (Screwtape) and a rookie demon (Wormwood). Wormwood is trying to capture his first "patient's" soul for the devil. Screwtape explains The Law of Undulation for Wormwood - how humans go through peaks and troughs with any type of commitment. Screwtape goes on to explain how to exploit the peaks and troughs.

Humans experience these peaks and valleys in all of our commitments - relationships, jobs, faith, exercise, etc. The first step in dealing with burn out is recognizing that if you are in one of these troughs it will soon go away. Don't make any rash decisions because you are frustrated or bored at the moment. Logically evaluate your position. Maybe it really is time for you to move if your job is getting stagnant.

My first year in my career, your Aunt Sara and I took a two week vacation to Spain. A few years later we took a train from Minneapolis to Seattle and then spent a week kicking around. Awesome vacations. I didn't have to look at email or check my voicemail. I had closure with my projects before I left and life went on without me.

I want you to take a vacation to get your mind away from the daily grind. Don't take your Blackberry with you. Relax and enjoy yourself. Then when you get back to work for a few weeks you can think through if you are in a trough that will transition to a peak OR if you are stagnant and need to make a change. Please use this strategy through the rest of your life. Americans are bad at taking vacations and we suffer for it.

We can chat about whether or not it is time for you to move on in a month or two. You need to logically evaluate where you are.

We naturally undulate between peaks and troughs in our careers. Don't make any rash decisions while in a trough.

Uncle Mike

Mike Smith ● White Owl Consulting ● 612-555-5550
100 Main St, #310, Minneapolis, MN 55411 ● www.WhiteOwlConsulting.com

From: msmith@whiteowlconsulting.com
Sent: Tuesday, May 1, 2012 4:42 PM
To: cdoe@acme-associates.com
Subject: **Death by PowerPoint**

Chris,

I'm proud of you! It's great that you are going to speak to the college group. Do them a favor and don't do the "normal" bullet point list presentation. You know the kind I am talking about. The one where the speaker comes to the head of the room. The lights are turned off. The laptop is fired up. PowerPoint is opened. The speaker starts to go through the first slide (go through is actually a kind way of saying he is reading it). That's a good thing, because he managed to fit about 500 words onto a multi-leveled outline. You can't make out a single word. It looks like the bottom lines on an eye chart. Is that some type of modern art? Only 40 more slides to go. WOW - now his bullet points are slowly fading on the screen. Is he going to make the text do loopty loops? You start daydreaming. Then you start hallucinating. It sounds like he is reading random passages out of Moby Dick. He looks and sounds like Ben Stein - Bueller, Bueller, Bueller. Now you are out cold and drooling.....

I know you've been to at least one of these presentations. Unfortunately the majority of them are like this. We professional types have been sucked into bullet point nirvana by years of using the default slide design in PowerPoint. Vice-presidents of Fortune 500 companies even congratulate each other on putting together a great "deck."

If you want to see the opposite type of presentation, go to Ted.com. You'll find a presentation on a topic that interests you and it will be well delivered.

A side note on your speech, make sure you are the right person to give the speech. If the speech is outside your area of competency, politely turn down the invitation. Obviously, your boss telling you to give the speech overrides this advice (but you should bring up your reservations if you don't feel you can handle the topic properly). Once you decide you can and should talk about the topic, take a breath and relax. You will most likely be speaking to people who know less about the topic than you do. This should definitely be true after you have done the research for your speech.

The first step in developing your speech is to organize the information you are going to convey. Don't open PowerPoint yet! Think about your audience and make sure your speech is geared to them. A speech to the local Rotary Club on climate change is going to be radically different than a climate change speech given to a group of professors who specialize in climate issues. Even if you think you know the audience, talk to the person who invited you to make sure you understand the group's expectations.

Now that you are thinking about your audience, use a pencil and paper to start brainstorming the information you should include in your speech. Maybe you could even put ideas on post it notes on a wall. Move things around until you develop a structure for the ideas you want to convey. You should develop a logical outline that covers your high points. Try to organize your talk into three overarching ideas and subgroup supporting information in groups of threes. For some reason, human beings easily remember groups of three (stop, drop, and roll or I came, I saw, I conquered).

Often the hardest part in developing a speech is stripping away all of the non-essential information. To put a limit on your speech, Guy Kawasaki (a seasoned marketing guru – early pioneer at Apple, author, venture capitalist, and serial entrepreneur) recommends presentations should follow the 10/20/30 rule. Ten slide maximum, 20 minute maximum, and 30 point font minimum. This is a great formula for giving a great presentation. You won't bore or confuse your audience, but this framework should allow you to deliver your message.

Organize your thoughts before you open up PowerPoint.

Uncle Mike

Mike Smith • White Owl Consulting • 612-555-5550
100 Main St, #310, Minneapolis, MN 55411 • www.WhiteOwlConsulting.com

From: msmith@whiteowlconsulting.com
Sent: Monday, May 7, 2012 8:21 PM
To: cdoe@acme-associates.com
Subject: **Re: Death by PowerPoint**

Chris,
I am glad you took a few days to develop your thoughts. Your outline looks good to me.

I hope you are thinking of your presentation as a story. The more anecdotes you can throw in, the easier it will be for your audience to pay attention. Humor is ok, but it has to be relevant to your speech. Avoid the common advice to start with a joke. You have been asked to give a professional presentation because you are an expert. They would have invited a comedian if they wanted humor.

Now that you have your thoughts organized, the second step in putting together your presentation is developing the slides. Again, stick with your pencil and paper. Take a blank piece of paper out for each slide. Translate the points from your outline into a sketched "story board" of your slides. I don't care if you can't draw, I can't either. You don't need to let anyone else look at it. Just draw things out so you understand them. The goal is to minimize words on your slides (remember 30 point minimum font size). It's even better to have no words - just a picture.

Dr. Albert Mehrabian did ground breaking research at UCLA that documented we remember about 7% of what we read as text, 38% of what we hear, but 55% of what we see as visual pictures. Use great photographs because your audience will remember more of your message. Don't use amateurish clip art. Go to istockphoto.com or gettyimages.com and spend a few bucks downloading professional photographs that will add a lot of pop to your presentation.

Now you are ready for step three – you can finally open Keynote, PowerPoint, etc. to start building your slides. Keep it simple. Use a black background with white text because it is the easiest combination to see and you won't shock your audience as you move through your slides. Don't use any moving parts. No outlines or bullet points. Use a serif font like Arial because they are easier to read on the screen. Limit your text to a few words per slide if you can't come up with a photo.

As with all good design, simplicity is the goal. The photographs and words (one or two words alone become an image) will support your speech. You don't want to do anything to distract from your message. Things in red add emphasis while things in blue are de-emphasized. Use color as well as "white space" to your advantage. You should plan on talking for thirty seconds to two minutes per slide.

Proofread the few words you use. You won't look like a professional if you have typos or bad grammar. It is a good idea to get someone to double check the presentation for you as a quality control check.

Spend time designing PowerPoint slides that will emphasize your message.

Uncle Mike

Mike Smith ● White Owl Consulting ● 612-555-5550
100 Main St, #310, Minneapolis, MN 55411 ● www.WhiteOwlConsulting.com

From: msmith@whiteowlconsulting.com
Sent: Wednesday, May 16, 2012 7:18 AM
To: cdoe@acme-associates.com
Subject: **Re: Re: Death by PowerPoint**

Chris,
I like your slides! I even liked your short bullet point list (rules can be broken) – key was using a couple of words per bullet point.

Toastmasters is teaching you the basics of putting together a speech and answering questions off the cuff. Now you need to graduate to being a PowerPoint user.

Step four in developing your speech is practicing your delivery. I don't like this part. It makes me feel like an idiot talking out loud, but I do it and you should too. I even force myself to practice in front of a mirror so I can work on my body language. If this is a make it or break it type presentation, you should even videotape your rehearsal so you can refine your delivery. Do the math – talking to fifty people for half an hour (adding in fifteen minutes drive time each way) adds up to fifty hours people are investing in hearing your speech. You owe it to them to practice for a few hours so you don't waste their fifty hours.

Practice with a handheld remote/laser pointer to control your slides (go buy one if they don't have one at work you can use). You don't want to stand at the laptop pushing the arrow buttons. Get comfortable blanking out the screen with the appropriate button on the remote. Occasionally shutting off the image really draws attention to what you are saying. But don't forget to turn PowerPoint back on.

You need to give your presentation out loud at least three times. This is on top of running through the presentation in your head. You want to memorize your talking points. Don't memorize a speech word for word because you will end up forgetting something and it will throw you off while you're delivering the speech. If you do manage to recite a fully memorized speech, you will end up boring your audience. You'd lose your enthusiasm and your audience would feel that.

So what if you forget a minor point? My eight year old daughter was telling me how she mixed up a few words while reading out loud to her class. I asked if that threw her off and she told me it didn't because the class didn't know what the words were supposed to be. She hit the nail on the head. Your audience won't miss a beat if you skip a minor item.

So, you develop a good speech, have slides that add punch to your message, and you'll practice enough so you are comfortable with your presentation. Even with all of this, you are still going to have butterflies in your stomach. I still get them with every speech. The good news is that your butterflies will be manageable because you are the expert and you are fully prepared. They'll go away once you start your speech.

What about show time? If you are being introduced, supply the introducer/moderator with a four bullet point highlight of who you are and a two sentence descriptive introduction to your presentation. Set yourself up as the expert through the introduction. Try to have the lights on. You need to be amazingly riveting to keep an audience awake in a dark room. Don't chance it.

Hopefully your presentation is in the morning. If at all possible, avoid the doldrums of mid-afternoon when a lot of people should take a siesta. Try to set up your laptop in front of you so you can see it while you are giving the presentation. You should focus on looking at your audience, not the screen. Don't turn your back on the audience to look at the screen behind you. If possible have a clock by your laptop so you can keep track of your time. Try to end ten to twenty percent ahead of schedule. Leave them wanting more, not looking at their watches wishing you were done.

Don't apologize if you have any missteps; just keep going through your presentation. Even if the projector blows up, you have practiced enough that you can give the speech without your slides. Relax and think of how great it will be when you are done!

Practice, practice, practice and then shine!

Uncle Mike

Mike Smith • White Owl Consulting • 612-555-5550
100 Main St, #310, Minneapolis, MN 55411 • www.WhiteOwlConsulting.com

From: msmith@whiteowlconsulting.com
Sent: Thursday, June 8, 2012 7:57 PM
To: Chris@gmail.com
Subject: **Time to Go?**

Chris,
Congrats! I can't believe you have been working for three years already. Now that you are back from vacation and mellowed out, it is time to think about your next career move.

In *Outliers*, Malcolm Gladwell spends a chapter describing that it takes about 10,000 hours of practice to become a true expert at a complex task. This time threshold is a good predictor of separating hobbyists from virtuosos. According to Mr. Gladwell's calculations, it is about the same amount of time Michael Jordan spent in the gym and Tiger Woods spent at the driving range.

10,000 hours is a lot of time. The vast majority of people get bored and taper down their practicing well before they reach that mark. Unless you have innate talent, it is also easy to get discouraged well before the 10,000 hour mark.

Now what does this mean for you as a professional? It's great news! You have somewhere between 1,000 and 2,500 hours a year to work on your craft. This depends if you are willing to put in time after hours and how much you get out of those hours at work. So, in four to ten years you should be a true expert in your field having put in the required time.

I'm going to expand on the sports analogy in a few ways that related to my career. In traffic engineering there are a host of skills needed to be an expert. I need to be able to do forecasting, use different modeling software, design traffic signals, do safety studies, understand road geometry, etc. Now I don't need to spend 10,000 hours in front of a specific model to be an expert traffic engineer. The same way Michael Jordan wouldn't be the greatest if he only practiced shooting baskets. He needed to learn to dribble, pass, rebound, play defense, etc. By practicing all of these inter-related skills he was able to become an expert the same way my set of traffic engineering skills are inter-twined.

More on the sports analogy - you refine your skills by having different coaches. Tiger Woods' dad first taught him to play golf. His dad's teaching was good enough to get him on The Tonight Show with Johnny Carson as a youngster. It would be ridiculous to think though that Tiger would become the most dominant golfer ever if he never had another coach. Similarly, Michael Jordan learned different skills by working with different teams/coaches - high school, college, and the pros.

So here is the advice your boss is going to yell at me for giving. You need to work with different "coaches" and "teams" to become a true expert at your profession. You should leave companies (or at least departments) every two to four years to work with a new coach who will teach you brand new skills as well as show you different angles on the skills you have acquired (i.e. go from dribbling to developing a cross-over move, learn zone defenses in addition to man to man defense).

You'll get to a point where most of your work feels routine. If you stay in the same position too long, you'll be singing the same song over and over again (with slightly different verses each time). When things start getting really redundant is the point at which you should leave. Make sure your next move expands your skills. If your boss taught you how to putt really well, your next boss should be an expert on driving the ball.

You should work for at least three different bosses while you are putting in your 10,000 hours. Each one should have significantly different areas of expertise in your profession. If you are an architect, maybe your first job focuses on building interiors, your second on building exteriors, and your third on the site planning. Once you have your 10,000 hours you are ready to stand on your own two feet. Maybe you'll be a partner leading your own team at a consulting firm or you'll be leading a department at your company. This is the time when you should be leading the design of the whole building.

One caveat, if you want to be the president/CEO of your company you will typically need a long tenure if you are trying to run a small to medium sized consulting firm (less than 300 people). These sized consulting firms promote within. If you have that type of goal in mind, I suggest you settle into a company for the long haul before you are ten years into your career. You'll need at least ten years with the company before you are promoted to the highest levels of management.

If you are settling into a routine at work, it's probably time to move on.

Uncle Mike

Mike Smith ● White Owl Consulting ● 612-555-5550
100 Main St, #310, Minneapolis, MN 55411 ● www.WhiteOwlConsulting.com

From: msmith@whiteowlconsulting.com
Sent: Sunday, June 17, 2012 3:34 PM
To: Chris@gmail.com
Subject: **Job Hunting**

Chris,
The best time to find a job is when you have a job. There is less stress on you to land something, so you'll perform better in the interviewing process. You are also in a better negotiating position because you aren't desperate. Some companies might find you more attractive too. The first question most people ask an unemployed candidate is "what happened at your last job." It can be a red flag.

You should look at the online job boards, your college placement office, professional society publications, and look at the websites of companies where you'd want to work. If you find any interesting leads through those sources, I want you to track down someone you can talk to at the potential employer. Use your network, LinkedIn, etc. to talk with someone outside of the HR department. You want to find out what kind of company it is and what they look for in a candidate. Get the inside scoop on the position.

Don't stop with the want ads though. Be proactive. Use the network you have been cultivating. Call your friends and ask them if they've heard of any opportunities. If there is a company you think you'd like to work for, call one of your contacts there and tell them you are thinking about leaving Acme. Ask them if they know of any opportunities within their company. Many companies have a standing policy to hire talented people even if they don't have an immediate job opening. You only find out about these types of opportunities by talking to people in your network. With all of these phone calls, stress that you are only thinking about leaving Acme and you hope they'll keep your call confidential.

Be thorough and be persistent in your job hunt. Exhaust all of your resources to give yourself the maximum amount of opportunities. Try to schedule informal coffee/lunch meetings to talk about possible positions. These informal meetings are the best way to position yourself for a new job.

It is time to update your résumé. Highlight accomplishments, not tasks – i.e. "I prepared the documents that resulted in xx project being approved," not "I wrote a report about xx." Tailor a different résumé for each position you apply for. You need to find out what is important to that company and write your résumé in a way that shows you are the ideal candidate. If you aren't close to the ideal candidate, you are wasting your time going after the position. Of course, your résumé needs to be perfect (no typos). Send me your first draft when you get it done. Work hard to get a few job offers in hand and then we'll go through them.

It's easiest to find another job while you're still employed.

Uncle Mike

Mike Smith • White Owl Consulting • 612-555-5550
100 Main St, #310, Minneapolis, MN 55411 • www.WhiteOwlConsulting.com

From: msmith@whiteowlconsulting.com
Sent: Tuesday, July 17, 2012 7:35 AM
To: Chris@gmail.com
Subject: **Door #1 or Door #2?**

Chris,
Did you catch the twelve inning Twins game last night or have you been too busy job hunting? It was a great game.

You've been doing an amazing job with your search. It is great that you have three companies interested in bringing you on board. Do you remember the advice I gave you about working on the production line? I wanted you to be at the heart of how the company makes money with your first job. I think that is still true at this stage of your career. It is too soon to take an "in-house" position.

I believe you've weeded out companies you wouldn't want to work for. Do you like the corporate culture at each of the three companies? Are they doing interesting work and making money? Don't go to a company that will feel like a sweatshop. What do you think of the person who would be your boss (hopefully you have a sense of what a bad boss looks like after your experience with your first boss). Your new position should stretch your skill set. You should take on more responsibility.

Remember, you are in the driver's seat. You don't have to leave Acme. Wait for the right opportunity. Don't burn any bridges though. Politely tell people you aren't interested as soon as you have decided their company isn't in the running.

Lastly – the money and benefits are important. Don' take less salary than you are currently making. Each job sets up your future salary. You should get at least a 20% bump in pay with your next job. Negotiate hard with the company you want to work for. They have a lot invested in you already and you are in a strong position. You can always walk away. Make a counter offer just to see what they say.

Realize the strength of your position and negotiate for the salary you deserve.

Uncle Mike

Mike Smith ● White Owl Consulting ● 612-555-5550
100 Main St, #310, Minneapolis, MN 55411 ● www.WhiteOwlConsulting.com

From: msmith@whiteowlconsulting.com
Sent: Saturday, July 21, 2012 2:04 PM
To: Chris@gmail.com
Subject: **How to Quit**

Chris,

You've lined up a great opportunity. You did well negotiating a higher salary with your number one choice. I'm glad they matched the higher offer from the other company (they didn't need to know the other company wasn't your top choice).

Management at Acme is probably going to try to talk you out of quitting. This is standard practice for good employees (and you are a great employee). They might throw a little money at you. But, I think taking back your resignation is almost never a good idea. You have emotionally convinced yourself you need to move on and it's going to be very difficult to get all of those reasons for leaving out of your head. Most of the people I know who are talked into staying end up leaving anyway in a year or two. Make up your mind. If you are going to quit, do it.

Here's how to quit professionally - its general business practice to write a brief letter addressed directly to your boss when you quit. Don't send an email. Write a one or two paragraph letter saying you are quitting for a new opportunity. Tell her when your last day will be (at this stage in your career, two weeks notice is customary). Thank the company and your boss for the opportunity you were given.

Keep it short and sweet. You shouldn't tell them where you are going to work. You shouldn't give detailed reasons why you are quitting. Don't turn the letter into a manifesto on why your boss sucks or why the company sucks.

Before you turn in the resignation letter, make sure your files are in order. Make sure you copy any information on your computer or in your rolodex that you may want later. It's possible you could be escorted to the door within an hour or two after quitting. At a minimum you should assume you will be watched a little closer than normal.

We're having company over for dinner tonight. I gotta run. I'll have some more thoughts for you tomorrow.

Make sure you never burn a bridge.

Uncle Mike

Mike Smith • White Owl Consulting • 612-555-5550
100 Main St, #310, Minneapolis, MN 55411 • www.WhiteOwlConsulting.com

From: msmith@whiteowlconsulting.com
Sent: Sunday, July 22, 2012 4:18 PM
To: Chris@gmail.com
Subject: **How to Quit - Continued**

Chris,
More thoughts on quitting –

So, once you have written your letter and have your files in order, I recommend you quit on a Friday (preferably after lunch). It will give you a breather before all of your co-workers stop by to ask what is going on and will also give you the weekend to come down from the stress of quitting (it will be stressful).

As far as how to quit - seal your letter in an envelope, walk in to your boss' office and give it to her. Tell her this is your resignation letter, that you have enjoyed working for her, and you appreciate the opportunities she has given you. Keep it brief. She will probably ask you where you are going. You should be honest and briefly explain the opportunity. As a human being, it will help her cope with your quitting. Also, if you are aloof the company might think you are stealing secrets and going to work for the competition.

If you are due for a bonus or your stock options are coming up, wait a few weeks. Look out for you and time your leap. These things are supposed to be rewards for past performance, but your employer will likely be motivated to short you if they can. They look at bonuses as a way to keep you, which is really deflated if you just resigned.

You'll probably be catching your boss off guard. Quitting is a lot like breaking up with a girlfriend – expect them to be mad at you and irrational.

When I quit from one of my jobs, my boss Aaron went into a little tirade. He told me I was being impatient and that I should have communicated with him better. Apparently he didn't see my resignation coming. I wasn't ready to be rebuffed and I don't think it was appropriate for him to start flying off the cuff (but he is human). It did confirm that it wasn't the right position for me though.

I am impatient, which has served me well in my career. Most successful people are impatient. They make things happen. I wouldn't have started my own firm when I was 28 if I wasn't impatient and I've never regretted going on my own. So be prepared for your boss to be irrational. Smile and thank them for the advice and leave their office as soon as possible. It is not the appropriate time to have a long discussion.

Send a quick email to the co-workers you work closely with as a courtesy. You don't want to burn bridges by having someone you're close to find out you quit through the gossip mill. Also, don't ever slander anyone or the company during the quitting process (or ever for that matter). Make sure you celebrate that night!

Quitting 101 – be calm, be cool, and be professional.

Uncle Mike

Mike Smith ● White Owl Consulting ● 612-555-5550
100 Main St, #310, Minneapolis, MN 55411 ●. www.WhiteOwlConsulting.com

From: msmith@whiteowlconsulting.com
Sent: Friday, July 27, 2012 4:51 PM
To: cdoe@acme-associates.com
Subject: **Congratulations!!!**

Chris,
I expected your boss to be upset. You are good at what you do and she
will miss you. You leaving makes her job harder. You did the right
thing for your career. Take Christy out tonight.

Celebrate your victories!

Uncle Mike

Mike Smith • White Owl Consulting • 612-555-5550
100 Main St, #310, Minneapolis, MN 55411 • www.WhiteOwlConsulting.com

From: gadams@acme-associates.com
Sent: Saturday, August 18, 2012 3:19 PM
To: kim99@gmail.com
Subject: **How's it going?**

Kim,
I'm glad you're doing well in Chicago! How was your first trip to Wrigley Field last night? Too bad the Cubs lost.

It is always a challenge moving to a new town AND starting a new job. It's exciting though and you have a great opportunity. You landed with a solid company. That's so important in this tight economy.

I am excited you like the idea of me being a mentor/sounding board for you. I feel bad I wasn't more helpful while you were in college. Reading those emails I told you about really opened my eyes about what it means to be a good uncle. Feel free to email me about anything. If you are in a crisis at work, call me on my cell phone.

In the meantime, here are a few thoughts for you based on those emails between Chris and his uncle –
1. Don't be the bottleneck. Whenever you are working as part of a team, get your work done as fast as possible so you aren't holding up the work others are doing.
2. Perception matters. You need to look and act like a professional. Wear nice clothes. Don't gossip. Don't get drunk with your co-workers. Your reports and memos need to have color, graphics, pictures, etc. Everything should reinforce that you are a professional.
3. Take good minutes. People don't like taking minutes, but they are very important in documenting decisions. Early in your career, others will see the minutes you take but probably won't see a lot of your other work products. Minutes are an opportunity for you to shine.
4. Small talk is important. Everyone has something to teach you. Practice asking questions that will get people talking. Then be quiet and listen. Be interested in what they have to say.
5. Speak up. You don't want to be seen as a wallflower. If you don't talk, you're co-workers may assume you have nothing to say.

6. Focus. Tackle the most important thing on your to do list immediately in the morning. Leave your less strategic, administrative work for the afternoon when your circadian rhythms are making you groggy. Don't waste time hanging out at the coffee pot. Limit checking your email to once in the morning and once in the afternoon. Plan tomorrow before leaving the office today.

I'll expand on all of these ideas in subsequent emails. Email me questions as you run into problems (which we all do!). **I'm here to help.**

Uncle George

George Adams

President
Acme Associates
50 South 6th Street, Suite 3245
Minneapolis, MN 55416
612-333-3333

Acknowledgements

I wouldn't have written this book without the encouragement of Andy Lawrence, Jenni Lawrence, and Jane Spack. On top of believing in the value of what I had to say, your review of my *rough* draft vastly improved my style and format. And thank you for your continued efforts in editing the manuscript.

Kathy Spargo, my right hand, also had a great impact on this book. You do a phenomenal job of improving my work and making me look better than I possibly could on my own.

Thank you to the members of the Business Book Club (Bryant Ficek, Bob Klingel, Andy Lawrence, Tim Lawrence, Lance Stendal, Kevin Stewart, and associate member Chris Spargo) who reviewed my second draft and made great recommendations. Our monthly business book discussions over the last four years have significantly influenced my thinking on careers and business.

Lastly, thank you to the countless business book authors who have shaped my thinking on careers and business.

Index

Made in the USA
Charleston, SC
23 January 2011